“I love a good story. *The Good Dad Gu* … a
better dad—encouragement with a g … .”

author of … *Smart Stepdad*

“Becoming a dad is one thing—*being* a dad is many things. If you want to be good at it every day and in every way possible, Charles Marshall can help you. If you’re like me, you learn best through stories, and there’s plenty in these pages that will drive home the wisdom that, when applied, will bless your children.”

Steve Chapman
author of *A Look at Life from a Deer Stand*

“If you’ve ever longed for fathering support from a dad who is right there with you in the trenches, *The Good Dad Guide* is for you. In this powerful and practical handbook, Charles Marshall initiates candid conversations about the challenges and the rewards of being an invested dad. With engaging stories with a dash of clever humor, this book serves as a road map for fathers who need someone to teach them what it actually looks like to lead and love their children well.”

Michelle Watson, PhD, LPC
author of *Dad, Here’s What I Really Need from You*

The Good Dad Guide reads like a roadmap for being the best dad you can be. This book will help you stay on the right road—and out of the ditches. Practical advice. Powerful stories. Encouraging insights. And an easy read. Take *The Good Dad Guide* for a test drive, and enjoy the ride!

Tim Shoemaker
speaker and author of *Super Husband, Super Dad*

THE GOOD DAD GUIDE

CHARLES MARSHALL

Cover by Rightly Designed

Cover image © Oksana Kuzmina / Adobe Stock Images

Published in association with MacGregor Literary, Inc.

This book contains stories in which people's names and some details of their situations have been changed.

THE GOOD DAD GUIDE

Published by Harvest House Publishers
Eugene, Oregon 97402
www.harvesthousepublishers.com

ISBN 978-0-7369-6528-6 (pbk.)
ISBN 978-0-7369-6529-3 (eBook)

Library of Congress Cataloging-in-Publication Data
Names: Marshall, Charles W. (Charles Wesley), author.
Title: The good dad guide / Charles Marshall.
Description: Eugene, Oregon : Harvest House Publishers, 2016.
Identifiers: LCCN 2015051272 (print) | LCCN 2016015050 (ebook) | ISBN 9780736965286 (pbk.) | ISBN 9780736965293 (ebook)
Subjects: LCSH: Fatherhood.
Classification: LCC HQ756 .M3444 2016 (print) | LCC HQ756 (ebook) | DDC 306.874/2—dc23
LC record available at https://lccn.loc.gov/2015051272

Printed in the United States of America

16 17 18 19 20 21 22 23 24 / BP-SK / 10 9 8 7 6 5 4 3 2 1

This book is dedicated to the many men
I've been privileged to know who have
modeled the best of fatherhood.

Acknowledgments

I know with great certainty that I wouldn't have seen the success that I have without the love and support of my wife and best friend, Laura Marshall. She is a gifted writer, loving mother, giving wife, and wise business partner. I'm profoundly grateful to have her.

I'm honored to once again work with Gene Skinner as my editor. Gene is a man of rare character, faith, and ability. I value and appreciate his many contributions toward making this a better book.

Bob Hawkins and Larae Weikert are living examples of business people who are ruled by Christian principles. When I first met both of them and began discussing the possibility of a relationship with Harvest House Publishers, I was struck by their humility and genuine spirits. I greatly appreciate the time and interest they have invested in me.

Chip MacGregor is known as one of the most respected and knowledgeable agents in the industry, but I mainly think of him as a friend. I love getting to spend time with him when we get the chance, and I am thankful for the many personal and professional contributions he has made in my life.

I wish my father, Fred H. Marshall, were still on this earth. I miss him constantly, and his contributions to my life and this book are too numerous to count. I think he would get a kick out of reading this book, and I look forward to sharing it with him one day.

Like countless other dads, I believe that my children are the best kids on the planet. Not a day goes by that I don't thank God for placing them in my life. They constantly teach me how to try harder, reach further, stand stronger, and love deeper.

Contents

Introduction

Becoming a dad is the best and most exciting thing that can happen to a man. Nothing else I've ever experienced has even come close. It's better than being a published author. It's cooler than receiving a standing ovation. It's more awesome than getting a big paycheck. It's more exciting than traveling and seeing famous landmarks. It is better than doing television or radio interviews. Seeing the faces of my children, hearing them laugh, and hanging out with them feeds my heart in a way that none of that can.

Having kids changed me in ways that I couldn't even imagine before I had them. It changed how I live and where I live. It changed the way I drive and where I park my car. It changed the reason I get out of bed in the morning. It changed what I pray and how I pray. And most of all, it changed my perspective.

Many years ago, before I was a speaker, I worked as an independent musician, traveling around the Southeast doing concerts at small churches. Back then my wife and I had no children and, as a result of my being a full-time musician, were poorer than church mice. Even when I did manage to make a few dollars, I had to invest that money in my career, buying more equipment or recording new music.

One day, when I was recording a couple of songs in an Atlanta-area recording studio, the studio owner started talking to me about the birth of his second child. He was obviously thrilled to have her and asked if my wife and I had any children. I told him that we didn't and weren't likely to anytime soon because we were so broke. He told me that having kids was awesome and encouraged me to trust God to take care of my family.

But having kids didn't look that awesome to me at the time. Fatherhood looked like a prison of responsibility, and I didn't want to get trapped. I had dreams. I didn't want to throw all of them away and become shackled with the drudgery of taking care of a family.

At the time, I couldn't see that I was scared and that I was being held captive by fear. Because I was fearful, I didn't take risks that would lead to growth and blessing. Like a slave clinging to his chains, I was holding on to dreams and desires that wouldn't compare to the freedom and fulfillment that being a dad would hold for me.

When my daughter was finally born, all of that changed in an instant. The dreams that seemed so enormously important before suddenly appeared trite and meaningless. They were small, brittle things that evaporated in an instant as my universe expanded exponentially. My world seemed limitless with possibility because it now contained a person worth fighting for. Knowing this little girl gave me purpose, strength, and resolve that I lacked before. Having a daughter saved me from becoming caught in the trap of myself.

Being a father has been the most wonderful, challenging, frightening, fulfilling, beautiful, and revelatory experience I have ever encountered. There have been many times I have literally gotten down on my knees and thanked God that I didn't miss out on being a dad.

This book is a celebration of fatherhood. My purpose in writing it is to encourage you, to let you know how important you are to the world. We fathers are told that we only exist for our genetic contribution in the creation of children—that everything else we are can be either duplicated or replaced by someone or something else. A bigger lie has never been told.

A father is a gift. He is crucial, vital, and indispensable. It is my prayer that this book encourages you to realize your importance and fulfill your potential as a dad. I hope you find in these pages the strength, knowledge, and empowerment you need to be the hero your child already believes you are.

Part 1

PROVIDE

My God will meet all your needs according to the riches of his glory in Christ Jesus.

PHILIPPIANS 4:19

1

A Tale of Two Laundrymen

Fred Bailey's occupation is listed in the 1930 census as "laundryman." In those times, working in a laundry was a fairly common profession. Men were needed to load huge amounts of clothes into giant washers and then transfer those wet clothes into industrial dryers that were several times larger than those found in today's Laundromats.

Then the Great Depression hit, and the laundry business plummeted. Fred lost his job, started drinking heavily, and then hit the road. No one was ever clear why he left his wife and five children. Some people said he was trying to better himself and his family's condition, so he traveled to other states in search of work. Some said he was a no-account bum who abandoned his family in their darkest hour.

About a year later his wife received word that Fred was dead.

Once again, details were sketchy and rumors abounded. Some folks said he was working a job with the phone company in Kansas and died when he fell off a telephone pole. Some whispered he was murdered in a back alley in Memphis for an unpaid gambling debt.

His family, of course, was devastated. His wife got a job and farmed out the kids to neighbors who were kind enough to watch them while she worked. The Bailey family struggled just the same as millions of other families did during that time. Clothes were handed down to younger children, feet went bare in the summer, and every spare penny was treasured.

But then a hero named Pop Wheeler showed up. Wheeler was also a laundryman and was working in a laundry the first time he became a hero. One of his coworkers had been working inside the drum of one of the huge dryers when someone accidentally turned on the machine.

The man inside was tossed around like a rag doll while everyone surrounding the machine tried in vain to switch it off. It was clear to everyone that the man's life was in danger. His neck or spine could easily be snapped if nothing were done. Acting quickly, with no thought for his own safety, Wheeler stepped forward and thrust his arm into the tumbling dryer, temporarily halting the tumbler while his coworkers pulled the repairman out. But arms aren't made to withstand that kind of force, and the dryer tore it from Wheeler's body.

The repairman's life had been saved, but Wheeler had lost his arm and could no longer work at the laundry.

Sometime later, Wheeler met the widow Bailey, and they became romantically involved. They married, and Pop Wheeler raised the widow's five kids as his own, making him a hero for the second time.

The youngest of the family was a little girl named Gwen who would grow up one day and become my mom. As I grew up, she would occasionally tell the story of her father, his drinking, and his abandoning her family. Like many of her generation, she didn't talk a lot about how that situation made her feel, but she left no doubt as to how her father's behavior impacted her family. She also left no doubt about how grateful she was that another man stepped up to become a father and provider for her family.

Back in those times, a man's career options were severely limited by the loss of an arm, but Pop Wheeler didn't use that as an excuse not to work. He found work doing whatever he could to provide for his adopted family, and as a result, they made it through one of the darkest economic times in our country's history.

The Takeaway

It is a father's responsibility to financially provide for his family. His effort—or lack of effort—will be remembered for generations to come.

2

Build a Boat

When I read *The Adventures of Huckleberry Finn* as a boy, I was transported to a world of freedom and adventure, riding the Mississippi River with Huck and Jim. I dreamed of building my own raft and setting sail on the Mississippi, just as Huck did, but my parents told me in no uncertain terms that the Mississippi River was not to be trifled with and enacting my plan would no doubt result in my untimely death. I took them at their word and came up with an alternative plan. I would still make a raft but would settle for a more manageable and less life-threatening body of water.

My main obstacle was that we were poor, but since that didn't seem to slow Huck down, I didn't see why it should be a problem for me. I drew a simple plan for a rectangular raft, with the main frame and supports built of two-by-fours and the top covered with plywood. I managed to scrape together enough two-by-fours for my project, but finding one sheet of four-by-eight plywood proved beyond me. So I moved on to Plan B, which was gathering about ten or twelve odd-sized smaller pieces of plywood and then cutting and piecing them together to make the platform for my raft. The finished product looked something like the paint job of the Partridge Family's bus.

But how would I make it float? My neighbor's dad owned a solid chunk of Styrofoam that measured roughly one foot by two feet by six feet, and I looked longingly over my fence at it every day. I begged my friend to ask his dad if I could have it, but his dad wasn't giving up that treasure for anything. Car or truck inner tubes would have been great, but those cost money too, and I was doing this project on the cheap.

I was stuck on this problem for a couple months, but then the jug of milk at the breakfast table caught my eye. Back then, all milk jug lids were screwed on, so I wondered if they would be airtight. Holding a few sealed milk jugs underwater a few times proved that they would work as flotation devices. Then I needed to figure out how much weight one milk jug would support and how many jugs I would need to float my raft. After a few more experiments and sketchy calculations, I had my number, which turned out to be just as many milk jugs as I could cram underneath the raft. After I spent a few weeks collecting all the milk jugs I needed, I fastened the jugs to the bottom of the raft with some old bicycle inner tube strips, and I was in business. I hauled/dragged/pushed the raft to a nearby pond and was thrilled to see that my raft floated quite nicely. I spent several afternoons floating around that pond, feeling like Huck Finn himself.

I learned at an early age to go ahead and start working on my dreams, but it seems a growing number of people these days prefer to wait. I know of a young father who remains unemployed because he's waiting for a big settlement check. He can't go back to work until he gets the check because it involves a work injury, so he does nothing. And he's done nothing for about five years now. His girlfriend, the mother of his child, goes to work and pays the bills.

I know of others who buy lottery tickets, hoping to win their way to financial stability. Others still collect unemployment benefits for years rather than take a job that is not in their field.

When I see situations like these, especially with fathers, I want to ask, instead of waiting for your ship to come in, why not build a boat? Instead of wasting years and years of your life when you have youth, energy, and opportunity, why not go ahead and get started building something? My first book, *Shattering the Glass Slipper*, is built largely on this one point.

Each family decides whether the mom will work outside the household. That is a separate issue. But unless the dad has some sort of disability, he needs to be working to keep his family financially afloat. It is a dad's job to provide for his family, no matter what he has to do to get it done. Barring the immoral or illegal, a dad needs to step up, gather whatever scrap pieces he has, and start building a life raft for his family.

The Takeaway

There is no excuse for not doing whatever you can to take care of your family. Instead of waiting for the perfect solution, start working with whatever you have at hand.

3

Real Men Empathize

My father was born on July 4, 1926, and belonged to the one-of-a-kind, never-to-be-equaled-or-replaced World War II generation. After surviving the hardship and struggle of the Great Depression, this entire generation willingly volunteered to go to war so they could protect their families and country from a great evil rising across the sea. My father joined the navy and served as a radio operator on a submarine. I believe at that time the mortality rate of men serving on submarines was somewhere around 50 percent. Like most veterans of that era, he was reluctant to talk about his actions in the war, saying only that he and millions of others just did their duty.

After the war, he attended the University of Georgia, where he played football and earned his degree. He landed his first job after college working as a high school football coach in the Atlanta area. He met my mom shortly afterward, started a family, and worked hard to put food on the table.

He had a lifelong passion for sports of all kinds. Whether it was football, baseball, basketball, or the Olympics—whatever and whenever sports were on—he was in front of our black-and-white Zenith, cheering loudly for his team.

Standing at six feet three and weighing about 220 pounds, he was a formidable and intimidating man. He was the type of guy who struck terror into the hearts of all my sisters' would-be suitors just by answering the door.

He wasn't hesitant to tell his kids he loved them, but he would never be caught talking about his daily struggles, such as our family's financial difficulties or the almost constant rejection he experienced when he transitioned into a sales career. In short, he wasn't an Alan Alda, touchy-feely, let's-all-hold-hands-and-discuss-our-feelings kind of guy. He was the kind of man who felt at home among men.

So it was a welcome surprise whenever he chose to express compassion for my little trials or hardships.

Back in the early 1970s, my family was deep in the depths of financial struggle. My father had a heart attack about that time and wasn't able to work, so my mother went back to work in the office of the Gibson's Discount Center on Highway 80 in Clinton, Mississippi. Money was scarce, and whatever luxuries we possessed, we had to earn.

My sisters and I were able to get work delivering the *Southwest Guide*, a local paper that was supported largely by the tons of ads that accompanied it. Every other week, a white van backed into our driveway and unloaded mounds of circulars, newspapers, fliers, and advertisements. It was then our job to haul them inside, separate them into stacks, and put one of each publication into a slim plastic bag to be distributed to each home in our area. My sisters and I then hung big canvas bags stuffed with papers on our shoulders and lugged them around town, hanging plastic bags on every home's doorknob. We would deliver all the papers in our canvas bags, go back home, reload our bags, and then head back out to deliver some more.

It was hard work for a ten-year-old under the best of circumstances. Walking for miles bearing a heavy load in the sweltering Mississippi summer was tough, but it was the wintertime that I found intolerable. The South rarely gets snow, but it does get cold—a damp, relentless, clinging cold. On one of those bitterly cold days, I returned home after delivering a load and began readying my bag to go out again. My father took pity on me and told me he would drive me back to the point where I had run out of papers. After we arrived, he drove the car along the street while I went from house to house delivering papers. From time to time I would warm myself in the car before getting out to deliver the rest.

But the thing that shines in my memory isn't that my dad came along and helped me out, as much as I appreciated him doing so. It was the look of concern and compassion on his face each time I returned to the car. He wasn't a man of many words, but what he had, he gave me.

"Son, I'm sorry you're having a rough time. I know how it is to have to be out in the cold and not be able to get any relief."

That is all I remember him saying, but that was enough. Just knowing that my father cared—that he had been through this type of trial and understood what I was experiencing—just that little bit was enough to get me through the ordeal.

That is the power of empathy. When your kids are having a hard time, they don't need a lecture. They don't need your advice. They don't need you to scold them. They don't necessarily even need you to rescue them.

What they need is your understanding. They need to know that you get what they're going through. And they need to hear from your own lips that you care.

Maybe you don't think telling your kids that you care is really you. I have to think that sort of thing wasn't really my dad either, but his was a generation that manned up and did the necessary thing whether they felt like it or not. And the empathy my dad showed me, not just that once but many times, remains planted in my soul today.

The Takeaway

A father's empathy and understanding provides emotional support and strength for his children. A little bit of understanding goes a long way with your child.

4

Chew on That for a Minute

Not long ago, I spoke to a gentleman who gives leadership speeches to people in the nuclear power industry. Since I'm always interested in growth and learning, I asked him to give me a couple of his top points. It surprised me a bit that one of his central themes was balancing work and family life in that stressful industry.

He said that most people in leadership in that field are under a lot of pressure at work, and their time is constantly in demand. That made sense to me. When there is a problem at a nuclear power plant, it needs to be handled right away. You can't really say, "Sorry the core is melting down, but I'm right in the middle of a video game with my kids. How about I handle it when I get back to work tomorrow?"

His advice was that men who have high-demand jobs should take extra care to create memories with their kids. Most of what we remember from our childhood consists of snapshots, really. Few of us can recall the day-in and day-out minutiae of growing up. Most of the things we remember were special to us in some way, so we need to make sure we plan special events for our kids, such as taking the family on outings, attending ball games, visiting theme parks, or going camping or fishing. His point was that by doing so, you are giving your children a lifetime of treasured memories.

That reminded me of the time my dad took our family on a fishing trip. My dad was many things, but an outdoorsman he was not. We had no boat, no rods, no equipment whatsoever, but Dad wasn't going to let that stop him. So, early one Saturday morning, Dad loaded all of us into our Oldsmobile Delta 88 and drove to Kmart, where my dad bought six cane poles, six snap-on floats, some fishing line, and pinch-on lead weights. Then Dad threw the fishing tackle in the trunk and tied the fishing poles to the door handles on the passenger side of the car. My mom, three sisters, and I had to climb in on the driver's side and scoot all the way over to the other side because the doors on the passenger side were tied shut. I can't imagine a policeman these days allowing a vehicle to roll down the highway with half the doors secured on the outside with bamboo, but apparently safety laws were a lot more relaxed in those times.

Dad cranked up the Delta 88, and soon we were flying down the road toward the Ross Barnett Reservoir with the cane poles slapping against the side of the car in the wind. After we arrived, we spent the better part of an hour trying to figure out how all the fishing gear was supposed to work. The rest of the day was spent casting our lines into the water, hoping that by some miracle we would catch something other than weeds and trash. Even so, it was a grand adventure that I'll forevermore be grateful to my father for giving us.

My point isn't that a little family excursion makes up for neglecting your family. It doesn't. It is every bit as important for a dad to be involved in the mundane as it is for him to be in the memorable, but that's just not always possible, is it? Sometimes the demands of life require that we are away from our families a bit more than we would like.

But that doesn't mean you can't still find ways to connect with your kids and build memories with them. It turns out that kids are pretty portable. You can take them with you practically anywhere—to the hardware store, to the post office, or even to work. When I was about four or five years old, my dad took me along with him on a sales call to visit a college football coach. Even as young as I was, I could tell that the trip was his way of sharing his passion for sports. As we drove through the campus, Dad enthusiastically pointed out the practice fields and giant football stadium. When we arrived at the coach's office, Dad visited with the head coach for a while, and then we were off again. On the way home, Dad bought me a pack of Wrigley's spearmint gum. Just me and Dad, chewing gum, driving down the road, alone together for the whole day—a priceless treasure I wouldn't sell for any amount of money.

Of course, you never know which memories your children are

going to be able to recall when they grow up, do you? The smart move is to load up their treasure chests with plenty of them. Because later in life, the main thing they're going to cherish isn't the fishing or the gum—it's the time they spent with their dad.

The Takeaway

Provide lifelong memories for your children by creating and scheduling special family activities.

5

Why Walgreens Dared to Do It Differently

In early 2013, I was getting ready to do the opening keynote speech for an association in the Northeast. The ballroom was rapidly filling up with people arriving for breakfast and the first session. As I sat at one of the front tables eating breakfast, the gentleman sitting next to me introduced himself as Randy and asked about my family. As we spoke with each other, I learned that Randy was also a family man and that we had several common interests.

Soon afterward, the program began, and I went up on stage to do my presentation. After I finished my talk, my host announced that Randy, with whom I had been speaking earlier, was going to be doing a session in another room. I felt a little embarrassed that I hadn't recognized a fellow speaker who was on the same meeting agenda as myself. Randy had been such an easygoing, personable guy that I had just assumed he was a staff member of the association. I apologized to him and told him I was looking forward to his presentation.

I got tied up talking to some folks in the main ballroom, so I arrived at Randy's session a little while after he had already begun his speech. Standing at the front of the room, Randy was showing the audience slides of his beautiful family: his wife, Kay, two daughters, Sarah and Allison, and their son, Austin. He told the story of how he and his wife had learned that their son was autistic and the struggles they had experienced raising him. He told of both the joy and the life lessons Austin had brought into their lives over the years.

As he spoke, it slowly dawned on me that I had heard about Randy before. I had seen a report on *NBC Nightly News* about him and his amazing accomplishments. This was none other than *the* Randy Lewis. In one of the most audacious and compassionate moves modern business has ever seen, he had envisioned and championed a project unlike any other. Working as a senior vice president for Walgreens, Randy proposed the building of one of the most efficient distribution centers in the world. But the thing that would make it truly unique was that one-third of the workforce would be staffed with people with disabilities of some kind. Employees with autism, cerebral palsy, Down syndrome, and missing limbs would be paid the same wages as coworkers without disabilities. They would receive the same benefits and be held to the same standards.

It was a ridiculous, absurd idea, much like going to the moon or eradicating polio. But it belonged to a man compassionate and determined enough to see the project become a reality. When he first announced his idea to a room of 5000 Walgreens store managers, he wasn't sure what response he would get. After his announcement, he was flooded with people asking him what they could do to help.

Today Randy's dream is a reality with not one, but two fully functional distribution centers—one in Anderson, South Carolina, and the other in Windsor, Connecticut. Both facilities are equipped with workspaces that are adapted to individuals' unique needs. They provide employment opportunities to many people who have never held jobs or had the opportunity to work. Having a job allows them to be self-sustaining and independent while building their self-esteem and confidence.

As I listened to Randy tell his story, I was deeply moved by his vision and courage. I was also profoundly touched because of my own family's struggle with my daughter's epilepsy. Listening to another parent talk about his struggles as a parent of a child with health challenges was a profoundly emotional experience for me.

I was moved, but I was also inspired. Randy's story is that of one person impacting the lives of thousands of people—one man allowing his own personal challenge to affect a positive outcome for others in similar situations.

After Randy spoke, he was gracious enough to do a book signing for his wonderful book, *No Greatness Without Goodness*. When I approached the table to get my own copy signed, I thought about telling Randy how much his story affected me. I thought of telling him about my own family's struggle with health issues. I thought about thanking him for all he has done for people with special challenges.

But when I got to the table and it was my turn to speak, I couldn't get a word out. I got so choked up, all I could do was nod my head and pat my heart with tears in my eyes. After a moment, I was able to collect myself enough to thank him and tell him how much what he's done means to me.

As a dad, it's my goal to provide a path for my kids, to do for my kids what Randy has done for his. I don't know that I'll ever create anything as grand as Randy, but it is my daily prayer that I will complete my mission of providing a solid path for my children that will lead to success and fulfillment in their lives.

The Takeaway

Dads have the opportunity and obligation to provide a vision and path for their children.

LOL Already

Our home is filled with laughter, but we had to work to get it that way. My wife will tell you that my son spent the first three months of his life crying. The whole time, from sunup to sundown, every minute of every day. I don't remember it that way, but my wife did all the heavy lifting during that time, so her opinion is the one that counts.

We eventually learned that the milk we were feeding him was upsetting his stomach. When we got him switched over to formula, he started feeling better, but his smiles were still rare. One reason might have been that we were living in a small house and he didn't have his own room. That was tough on him when he tried to sleep because he was sensitive to both light and sound. If the television was too loud or our voices were raised or a cricket was chirping a mile away, he would wake up and start crying.

So for his first year of life, his disposition was like anyone else's who hadn't had enough sleep. There were many days he was grumpy and irritable. Most of the time, he wore a shell-shocked expression that seemed to say, "What have I gotten myself into?"

When he was a year old, we moved into a larger house and he got his own room, and he was able to enjoy a full night's rest for the first time. But even then, he was a pretty serious little fellow. His temperament leaned toward the thoughtful and introspective. He loved being with the family, but after a while, enough was enough, and he wanted some alone time. We tried to accommodate his needs as much as possible, but it bothered me that my son didn't seem to see the upside of moving from his mom's warm, quiet tummy into our cold, noisy family.

I felt I needed to acquaint this little guy with the lighter side of life—to teach him that this world can be a pretty awesome place if you don't take it too seriously. I launched a campaign to play, kid around, and joke with him whenever I could. For years, I tried to show him "the funny" wherever and whenever it popped up.

I was careful not to make him the butt of any jokes though. You don't learn humor by being picked on. You only learn to resent the one telling the joke. Instead, we looked for humor elsewhere. When things went wrong—when the dog did something unusual, when we weren't on time, when the food spilled—I tried to help him through the ordeal by showing him that it wasn't the end of the world.

God gave us the gift of humor not only to help us enjoy life but also as a defense against its many woes. Trust me on this. Life is serious enough. You don't need to look for the depressing. It will come looking for you. You won't need to wait for disappointment. It will show up soon enough. If you want some pain, just hang out for a moment or two and you'll get some.

Laughter, though, is a small miracle. It's one of those things that can turn a disaster into an adventure. When my kids were small, my wife used to come pick me up from the airport with them in the backseat. It takes every bit of an hour to get from my house to the Atlanta airport, but it can seem a lot longer than that with two small kids in the car.

One time when we were about halfway from the airport to our house, both kids had had enough and started the end-of-life-as-we-know-it wailing. Of course, that was about the time we ran into an impenetrable wall of traffic, so Laura and I had to sit in the car, creeping along at about two miles an hour, with two kids screaming at the top of their lungs. I was busy driving, so I asked Laura if there was anything she could do to get them to stop crying, but at that point she had exhausted her bag of tricks. She tried doing what she could, but nothing helped. Laura looked at me and I looked back at her, and we both would have given anything to be about six hours away from there on a beach.

But then a funny thing happened. We both started laughing. Something about the ridiculousness of our situation struck us, and we both let go. At first we chuckled, and then we howled until we had tears in our eyes. The kids were still crying, but we didn't care. We must have laughed for ten or fifteen minutes. I can't begin to tell you how it helped relieve the tension and get us home.

Dad, humor is one of your best tools in creating a peaceful household, so it's a good idea to stock up on it. Do what you can to cultivate an atmosphere of levity. Import it into your home. Watch a funny movie. Read a funny book. (My kids recommend *I'm Not Crazy, but I Might Be a Carrier* by that Charles Marshall guy.)

It might not sound like a big deal, but when you see what humor can do for your children, you will be amazed. Now my son has a great sense of humor. Often he is the first in the family to crack a joke. To hear him laughing at a comic strip or a book is poetry to my ears.

And when I hear that, I think, *I did that.* I helped give him something that will serve him for the rest of his life. And in the end, what more could a dad hope for than to give his child such a gift?

The Takeaway

Provide and encourage an atmosphere of lightheartedness and humor in your household.

7

I Love You with All My Internal Organs

A story came across my desk yesterday about a pastor who gave a life-changing gift to someone he barely knew. As he was praying for a man in his congregation who needed a kidney, the pastor felt the Lord was leading him to give the man one of his own.

I've heard similar stories before, and they always amaze me. That kind of selflessness is hard for me to imagine. If somebody asked me for a kidney, I'm not sure how I'd react. Mostly likely, I'd avoid eye contact and attempt a subject change.

Friend: "Hey, Charles, how about letting me have a kidney?"

Me: "Wow, is that Oprah on TV? Wonder what she's been up to?"

But I've met people who have made that decision. I was booked to speak at a banquet a couple of years ago and was talking to the other people at my table while waiting to begin my program. Somehow, the subject of kids came up, and the gentleman on my right told a story of some health challenges his daughter had when she was little. The couple sitting to my left nodded their heads in sympathy as he told his story.

"Yes, it's really hard to see your child suffering," the woman on my left said. "Our daughter had to have two kidney transplants, and it was very difficult seeing her go through all that."

"Wait a minute…two kidney transplants? Where did she get the kidneys?" I asked.

The lady's husband sitting next to her smiled at me in a sad sort of way and pointed at himself and his wife. "We each have only one kidney," he said. "She is missing one on her left side, and I'm missing one on my right."

I was stunned. "Are you both all right? Can you function okay with only one kidney?"

The husband and wife shared a smile with each other. The woman shrugged and replied, "It's what you do for your kids."

I used to wonder about this type of love when I was young. I saw my parents making sacrifices that I knew I couldn't make. I asked them how they could sacrifice for us kids, and they told me I wouldn't really understand until I grew up and had kids of my own.

Now I get it.

My daughter had her second grand mal seizure when she was seven years old, and I watched in horror as she slipped into unconsciousness and began convulsing. We called 911, and I rode in the back of the ambulance with her to the hospital. I stood beside her while expert hands tended to her in the ER, administering a sedative to short-circuit the seizure. I stroked her small head as she lay on the gurney and waited for what seemed like an eternity for her to wake up and say something, anything at all, so I would know she was okay.

I would have gladly traded anything I had—any material possession or any of my own organs—to help my little girl. And I'd do it right now. Because that's what parents do.

God changed something in me the day I became a father. I found something bigger than myself for which I would be willing to give my life. It's an honor to be a dad. And it's humbling knowing a type of love that makes me a better man than I would have been had I not become a father.

The Takeaway

Fathers have it within them to provide anything their children need, even if it means literally giving them parts of their own bodies.

Part 2

PARTICIPATE

Whatever you do, work at it with all your heart,
as working for the Lord, not for human masters,
since you know that you will receive an inheritance from
the Lord as a reward. It is the Lord Christ you are serving.

COLOSSIANS 3:23-24

8

Diaper War Stories

There are certain moments you always remember in your life: the day you graduate, the day you get married, the day you change your first diaper. Just after we got married, my wife and I decided to volunteer in the nursery at our church. Great idea, huh? Ah, we were young and foolish back in those days.

Surprisingly, things were going pretty well that first time. All the kids were happy. None were missing. Halfway through our shift, I discovered that kids will pretty much sit there and be quiet if you keep shoving Cheerios and Goldfish at 'em. Then I noticed an ominous odor coming from the direction of Allen Keppler's diaper. After investigating and confirming my suspicions, I reported my findings to my wife, who replied, "Finders keepers." So I rolled up my sleeves and waded in.

I don't remember a lot of details about the incident. I've done my best to repress the memory, but I do remember that Allen had given it his best shot. Taking pity on me, my wife came over and finished the job, probably because the sight of a grown man crying while changing a diaper was too much for her.

After the service, I walked up to Allen's parents and told them that Allen had dropped a big one. I might have also hinted that they owed me big-time.

That's when they told me I should have let them know and they would have come and changed the diaper for me. That's the kind of thing I would have liked to have known before I fought the Battle of Allen's Dirty Diapie.

Years later, we had our own kids, and diaper changing escalated to a whole new level. Both of my kids' diapers were like luxury vehicles. They always came fully loaded.

But here's the thing about changing your own kid's diaper. Even though it smells just as bad, it's just as yucky, and it's no more pleasant, you man up and do it, and it doesn't bother you quite as much. (Well, after a while it doesn't.)

Recently, I was standing around talking to a bunch of guys at a backyard barbecue. We were interviewing one of the guys about being a new dad, and he smiled as he related his diaper war stories. Then one of the guys whom I'll call Max spoke up and told everyone he hadn't changed one of his kids' diapers.

I looked at Max and said, "No way! Not ever? Not even one?"

"Nope," Max said with a proud look on his face. "I always had my wife take care of it."

You might think it strange, but I have to tell you that I felt a little sorry for Max when he said that. You see, it's not the mess that I think of when I remember those times. It's the countless moments of connection with my kids that come to mind. I think of the treasure trove of memories I bought by stepping up and changing those diapers.

I think of my son laughing as I sang the theme song from the old television show *Rawhide* to him.

> Rollin', rollin', rollin',
> Though the streams are swollen
> Keep them dogies rollin'
> Rawhide!

I would sing in my loudest, most operatic voice. He would dissolve in giggles, and I would laugh right along with him.

I'd sing worship songs to my daughter, and when she smiled her toothless, 300-watt smile at me, I felt like I was investing my life in something that mattered.

If you pull back from life because it's messy—if you shy away from interaction with your kids because it's uncomfortable—I would submit to you that you are walking away from treasure, that you are leaving life's most precious currency on the table. There are times when engagement with your kids is hard. There are times when, well, it just stinks, but it is in those times that you have the opportunity of the greatest reward.

The Takeaway

Every chore in taking care of your children is an opportunity to participate in their lives and connect with them.

9

Getting Shousy

My wife and I were out at a restaurant when we noticed that the kids at the next table were getting out of control. Of the three kids at the table, two were standing in their chairs, yelling at the top of their lungs, and the third was crawling under the table. The parents didn't seem to notice anything amiss.

After observing the chaos for a few minutes, I said to my wife, "Those kids sure are shousy, aren't they?"

My wife looked puzzled for a moment and replied, "What?"

Thinking she hadn't heard me, I repeated myself. "Those kids over there really are shousy, don't you think?"

My wife shook her head, the puzzled expression still on her face. "What do you mean?"

"You know, shousy—loud, out-of-control, boisterous...shousy."

She nodded her head and agreed that they certainly were boisterous.

A couple weeks later, I used the word "shousy" again, and once again she acted like she had no idea what I meant.

"Wait a minute," I said. "Are you telling me you don't know what 'shousy' means?"

My wife has a degree in journalism and worked as a newspaper writer for five years before we had kids. She's been playing word games since she could read. She's a holy terror playing Scrabble, and you don't want to make the mistake of jumping into the ring with her playing Words with Friends. So when she's unfamiliar with a word, it's kind of a big deal.

"I'm telling you I've never heard that word," she said. "Are you sure it's even a word?" she added with a smirk.

"Of course I'm sure it's a word!" I replied. "We used it all the time when I was growing up. It means loud, obnoxious, boisterous...kind of like those kids in the restaurant the other day."

"Okay, if you say so," she said.

"Look, I'll show you," I said, walking over and picking up a dictionary. I thumbed through the *S* section for about three or four minutes and couldn't find a trace of anything like the word "shousy."

"This is ridiculous," I said. "We used this word all the time growing up. I'm going to call Mom. She'll tell you it's a word."

I got my mom on the phone and told her my wife and I were having a disagreement about the word "shousy."

"Could you please tell her that 'shousy' is a real word?" I asked my mom.

Mom laughed and said, "Well, it was a real word to us."

I asked her what she meant, and she told me that a family with wild kids lived right down the road from us. Their last name was Shouse, so whenever the kids in our family were acting up and loud, my mom would say we were being "shousy" like the Shouse kids.

So for decades I had been walking around using a made-up word. Nobody had ever called me on it, so I didn't know the difference. I guess back then, I might have been embarrassed had I known I was misspeaking. But now the memory makes me smile because it's part of what made my family special growing up.

It's not just the achievements that make your family unique. It's all of the mistakes, oddities, misfires, and quirks that give a family personality. Those are the things you will cherish and fondly remember years from now.

With the creation of each new family comes an opportunity to create new traditions, new behaviors, and even new words. But you also have the opportunity to hold on to some of the old ones as well if you're so inclined.

So if your kids are getting kind of wild, you have my permission to tell them to calm down and not be so shousy. Or you can make up your own word and then laugh when your kids call you years from now to ask you what it means.

The Takeaway

A father's participation in his family will help create that family's uniqueness and personality.

10

A Purple Curse or a Prehistoric Blessing

As you enter parenthood, it is impossible to prepare yourself for the relentless onslaught of kids' music and videos that are thrown at you from every direction. Whenever you turn on the TV, you are assaulted with an endless barrage of Barney the Dinosaur, Dora the Explorer, and the Wiggles.

As far as I can tell, it looks like this is how it has always been from the beginning of time. Apparently Lincoln, Washington, and Moses all had to put up with it, so we do too. The parent-to-be always declares that he will never let that kind of stuff in his house, but everyone—and I mean *everyone*—eventually gives in. It's inevitable. It's like hair loss, weight gain, or bad eyesight. They're all going to happen. It's part of life, and there's nothing we can do about it.

And you know what? It's not all that bad if you lean into it a bit. You can make it work for you as a point of connection with your kids.

When my daughter was two or three years old, I would hear her laughing and singing in the next room while she watched Barney. I always listened for the end of the program, and then I'd dash into the room to catch the closing song. I stood right beside her and held her little hand, swaying back and forth, singing along with Barney, "I love you, you love me!" And at the "with a great big hug and a kiss from me to you," I would lean over and trade kisses and hugs with my girl. When my son came along, he wanted to be a part of it, so eventually the whole family was in the family room holding hands and singing.

Afterward, I'd go back to whatever I was doing, but just for a moment I got to connect with my kids in a meaningful way, and they loved it. So did I—it's one of my treasured memories that I wouldn't trade for anything.

Then along came the Wiggles, a singing group for kids that at one time was one of Australia's biggest exports. My kids would watch their videos over and over again as four guys in yellow, red, blue, and purple shirts sang about fruit salad, Dorothy the Dinosaur, and waving your arms like Henry. There is something about kids that enables them to watch the same program hundreds of times in a row and not grow sick to death of it. And of course, if the kids were watching the show, that meant one of us was at least hearing it for the umpteenth time. It got so bad, my wife and I could not only sing the lyrics of every song but also recite the dialogue from complete episodes. Don't tell the Wiggles, but the truth is, we got fairly sick of them.

Even so, when the Wiggles came to town, I dug deep and took my daughter to see them in concert. And I have to say, it was one of the best concerts I've attended! My daughter and I had a great time singing along with their songs, laughing as Jeff fell asleep in the back of the arena, and watching in amazement as Captain Feathersword did amazing flips through the air. We even stood up and danced a bit. And I hate to admit it, but I even got a little teary-eyed when Murray, Anthony, Jeff, and Sam (Greg was out sick) rolled out onto the stage in their Big Red Car, singing, "Toot toot, chugga chugga, big red car."

It was one of those moments that I knew I'd remember for the rest of my life. Sitting there with my daughter, experiencing something that was important to her. I still remember the expression on her face as she soaked in the wonderment of the show. I wouldn't have missed it for anything.

I know my wife and I sound like a couple of geeks, and maybe we are. But we're a family that takes every opportunity to show one another our love, so if that makes us geeks, then so be it. I'll take my loving, weird family over a cool, aloof family any day.

The Takeaway

The things that irritate you may actually be opportunities in disguise. Instead of pulling back from your child's world, jump in and be a part of the wonder.

11

Marshall's Law

The story goes that a man walked up to a beautiful woman in Walmart and said, "Excuse me. I can't find my wife. Would you mind talking to me for a minute or two?" When the woman asked why, he said, "I can never find my wife in this store, but whenever I talk to a beautiful woman, my wife shows up in about thirty seconds."

I've found this same principle to be true with kids. It has never ceased to amaze me that if I spill something in the kitchen, like milk or applesauce, my kids will come from miles around to walk right through it. I don't mean they'll get close to it. I don't mean they'll go near it. I mean their little inner GPS units will plot a course directly though the geographic center of the mess. Out of all the square footage available in your home, they will feel an immediate and irresistible urge to materialize and plod through your spill.

This principle is not restricted to the kitchen, but applies to any area, wherever you happen to be—the garage, grocery store, surface of the moon...wherever.

I was relating this principle at a party the other night when somebody spilled something on the floor and, so help me, a kid appeared out of nowhere and walked right through it as all the parents watched in amazement. I have to tell you, I looked fairly prophetic at that moment.

At such times, when I watch feet walking through the jelly on the floor and feel my blood pressure rising, I have to remind myself that the reason I have this particular floor in the first place is for little feet to walk on.

Family life is messy. People cause problems. But the life undisturbed is the life unlived. I think that sometimes when we dads try to run a tight ship, we need to remember that it is the voyage that matters, not the ship. One day the voyage will be just about over, and those little feet running through the house will have grown up and moved on to their own houses. Our homes will be shipshape and in order. But is that really all we're shooting for?

I think of all the grumpy old men I know who are rambling through their undisturbed, uninhabited homes right now, and I think that maybe I'm better off how I am. I don't want to wind up with my house in order because it's uninhabited. I don't want to be a man who is more comfortable in a tomb that he is in a kindergarten.

Then I think about the other guys I know whose homes are being invaded by the next generation with all the accompanying noise, activity, and mess, and I have to smile. I like the picture of the family patriarch being crawled on as he sits in his dad-chair. I like the idea of being part of the life of a home. And I know for certain that is the direction I'd like to point my ship.

The Takeaway

A lived-in home is a messy home (at least to some degree). Instead of just policing the activity in your home, join the party.

12

Get the Picture? Be the Miracle

Sometime in the middle of getting my kids' pictures taken at the portrait studio, it hit me. How could I have ever thought this would be a good idea?

My one-year-old son is crying his head off while his three-year old sister watches him, looking like she is about to start crying at any moment too. The photographer is doing her dead-level best to pull this airplane out of a nosedive and salvage something from this effort, but the more she smiles and wags squeaky toys in front of my son, the more distressed he becomes and the more he wails.

It seemed like a good idea at first. Everyone needs to go get their kids' picture taken at a studio, right? Then you take the pictures home, where they hang on the walls for the next 30 or 40 years. It's tradition. It's what parents do.

But it's got to be done right. It's like a military campaign. There are about a thousand things that can go wrong, and any one of them could torpedo your entire project. If the kids are cranky, if they're tired, if they're hungry, if they're fighting...the whole project fails and you don't get those happy smiles hanging up on your walls. So my wife studied the situation and made the appointment at the portrait studio for the precise time of day when the kids would be fed and well-rested.

We got to the studio right on time—and then waited for about an hour and a half while the photographer finished shooting another family. While we waited, my wife and I grew more and more stressed because we realized that the shelf life of our kids' great dispositions was rapidly running out. We had a narrow window to get the photos taken before the little folks started wearing out and getting cranky. After that, what can you do? You can't really yell at them or threaten them with dire consequences and then turn around and say, "Smile for the lady, kids!" How's *that* picture going to look hanging on the wall for the next few decades?

No, the best you can hope for is a miracle—that somehow even though the kids are tired, bored, and hungry, you're going to capture the very best of their radiant personalities on film. You hope that the photographer has some type of magic of which you are not yet aware that transforms disastrous situations into beautiful family portraits. After all, she's a professional. She's presumably trained for this kind of thing. Surely she has one or two tricks up her sleeve to salvage this kind of debacle.

But 30 minutes later, when my son is wailing like it's the end of days, I'm thinking that maybe I was wrong about her having any magic. Maybe I was wrong to do this whole thing. It makes sense now.

My three-year-old girl? Outgoing, never-meets-a-stranger extrovert. My one-year-old son? Completely the opposite. Introvert, bashful, hiding behind Dad's or Mom's leg whenever we encounter anyone new. Our plan had been to take this boy, this shy little fellow who clings to Mom in public, place him in a strange environment, sit him on top of a waist-high surface, back ten feet away from him, and let a complete stranger try to talk him into smiling. That just makes a whole lot of sense, doesn't it?

When we first put him on the table, he looked dubious, then worried, and then panicked. Then he moved into a full-on breakdown. And I'm standing there, thinking, *Why didn't I see this coming?*

But then the miracle happened.

As the photographer was jumping out from behind a curtain saying, "Boo!"—which, of course, only terrified my son even more—I had an epiphany. This is what dads are great at.

I do a lot of things for my kids at an acceptable level. I feed them, read to them, change them, and even bathe them, but truth be known, their mom does all those things better than me. The one thing I know I *can* do is be silly with my kids. I am the ta-da guy!

On top of that, I worked as an entertainer doing stand-up comedy for years. As I watched the photographer jumping out from behind a partition, trying to make my kids smile, I realized that what was needed was a quality entertainer and that I was exactly the man for this job.

I went behind the partition and said. "Where's Daddy? Where's Daddy?" and then leaped out with my biggest, "Here he is!" And can I brag for a second? My improv brought the house down. I absolutely slayed them. That two-person audience thought I was the funniest thing they had ever seen. I continued my performance and prayed the photographer would capture their reactions, and you know what? I've had those wide-open smiles hanging on my walls for about a decade now.

It's so easy to sit back and wait for the miracle, isn't it? But my experience is that God often uses us to answer the prayer. It's up to me to step up and do what I can. It's amazing how much can be accomplished if you jump in and do what you can now instead of waiting for the big answer to arrive.

I've found that a lot of times, the miracle we're all looking for is standing right in front of us in the mirror, or in some cases, jumping out from behind the curtain, saying, "Ta-da!"

The Takeaway

A father brings a unique and singular skill set to the family. It is up to him to assist his family with those gifts, however they may be needed.

13

Get Down Tonight

Theodore Roosevelt is the coolest president the United States has ever had, hands down, end of argument. He was the first president to travel outside the country while still in office. He was the first president to fly in an airplane, the first to ride in a car, and the first to refer to the presidential mansion as the White House. When he invited his friend Booker T. Washington to dinner, he became the first president to host an African-American at the White House. His help in negotiating the end of the Russo-Japanese War won him a Nobel Peace Prize in 1906.

He was born into a rich family, but he was poor in health. He struggled in his youth with asthma, severe headaches, intestinal problems, and poor eyesight. His father encouraged him to face his physical problems head-on by strengthening his body. Working a vigorous exercise regimen, he was able to compensate and overcome much of his physical weakness. He was an avid boxer, swimmer, hiker, and weight lifter.

As president, he strongly advocated for the preservation of forests, establishing five new national parks and creating the United States Forest Service. Which, by the way, is one of the main reasons you find his likeness carved into stone on Mount Rushmore, right alongside other presidential greats such as Washington, Jefferson, and Lincoln.

On October 14, 1912, Roosevelt was in Milwaukee, campaigning for a third term as a third-party candidate against incumbent William Howard Taft and Democratic candidate Woodrow Wilson. He was on a tight schedule and wasn't feeling well, so he planned on making only a brief appearance before moving on. As Roosevelt stood in his car, waving to the crowds, a man approached and fired a .38-caliber pistol at him at point-blank range. The bullet hit Roosevelt in the chest, and it was said that he didn't even notice he was shot until he reached into his coat and felt blood. Fortunately, the bullet was slowed by a copy of his speech and the steel eyeglasses case Roosevelt was carrying in his coat pocket.

The most amazing thing about this story is that Roosevelt refused to be taken to the hospital before speaking to the crowd. With a bullet embedded in his chest, he stood and delivered the speech for nearly 90 minutes in his blood-soaked shirt. Only afterward did he consent to be taken to the hospital, where he was treated for the next eight days.

As wonderful as all these accomplishments are, I think one of the best things about him was that he was a passionate and loving father. It is said that he readily joined in his children's pillow fights, played hide-and-seek with them, and even crawled on the floor with them in the White House, preferring a connection with his children over his dignity as president.

One of my favorite family pictures from my childhood is of my father lying on the ground with my sisters and me crawling on top of him. Rolling around on the floor with my kids has also been one of the most delightful parts of my own fatherhood experience. I love it when I see dads out in public getting down and playing with their kids.

If you are going to relate to your kids, you have to be willing to get down on their level both literally and figuratively, both in play and when the situation is more serious. Whenever you have something important to say to your little ones or whenever they have something important to say to you, you need to kneel, sit, or squat to get down on their level. If they are in their teens and are as big as (or bigger), half the job is already done for you. All that's left is for you to adjust your attitude to be on their level so that there can be an even exchange of thought and emotion.

When you make an eye-level connection with your kids, whether in fun or in the serious moment, you're bonding and strengthening your connection with them. But much further than that, you are living a moment that both you and your kids will treasure for the rest of your lives.

The Takeaway

Your kids would rather have you crawl on your knees than stand on your dignity. Drop down to their level and experience life from their viewpoint.

14

I'm Going to Need That in Writing

About a year after my mom passed away, my sisters went through her personal effects and began making the tough decisions about which sibling got what item. Dad had died years before, and now the burden of divvying up our parents' last possessions fell to my sisters. I didn't envy them the task. They had to go through and examine the contents of every box, every piece of furniture, and every old trunk. It took them an entire day filled with reminiscing, tears, and heartache just to get through a small portion of their belongings.

Mom had kept an old chest in her room since before I was born. I had never seen the inside of it, but at the bottom lay a two-page, handwritten letter. After reading the letter, my sisters discovered that on the day after my birth, my tough-guy, no-nonsense dad sat down and wrote a tender, heartfelt letter to my mom, expressing his love and profound appreciation for her giving him a second son. With every line, he poured out his gratefulness for this new boy and the hope he had for this child.

Maybe writing love letters to his sweetheart wasn't that unusual for my dad. Maybe he wrote a thousand others before this one and a thousand afterward. Or maybe this was the only one. I can't tell you. What I can tell you is that this was the first and last one I've seen, and I now count it among my most valued possessions. I have, in my father's own hand, words conveying his appreciation, not only for my mom but also for my arrival in our family. It means something to me to have a tangible, written declaration from my dad expressing his love for my mother and me. It's the only letter of any type from my father that I still have.

In Gary Chapman's bestselling book *The Five Love Languages*, he identifies the five different ways we express love. The five languages are words of affirmation, quality time, gifts, acts of service, and physical touch. Everyone has one love language that is most meaningful to them. But I believe there is something special, something enduring, about having someone you love take the time to communicate their feelings for you on paper. If that missive is in that person's own handwriting, it's even more special. A love letter can be held, touched, and seen over and over again. It's an experience that involves multiple senses and engages one's emotions.

Early on, when my daughter was only four or five years old, I found out that she enjoys communicating through love notes. Every so often, I would find special notes to me on my dresser—decorated with colored hearts, rainbows, and smiley faces—in which she poured out her love for her daddy. I made sure I thanked her for them and told her how much I appreciated them. She beamed at me and then casually mentioned that she would very much like to receive one of those notes herself. The very next morning she found a love note on her dresser from her dad, which she thanked me for and then hinted that the note might be even nicer if it had a bit of artwork like hers had. I made sure that every note afterward was decked out with my very best hearts and...well, that's it, really. Just the hearts. I can't draw much else, but I must say that my hearts are second to none. I draw them large, medium, and small, and I fill them in with a variety of colors. It seemed to do the trick with my daughter.

It wasn't long after observing these exchanges between his sister and me that my son wanted in on the action. With his notes the sentiments were the same, but the artwork wasn't as important to him, so he let me get by with doing a little less of it.

I don't know if they keep any of my letters. It doesn't matter to me one way or the other. I'm still going to keep writing them because I like feeding their young hearts with love and encouragement. There's nothing like a love note from your dad, and every child ought to get one at least once in their lives.

The Takeaway

Take the time and make the effort to communicate with your child in written form so that they may have a tangible expression of your love.

Part 3

PREPARE

We have all had human fathers who disciplined us and we respected them for it. How much more should we submit to the Father of spirits and live!

HEBREWS 12:9

15

The Shaky Saga

On the day my daughter was born, she received a beautiful flower arrangement from my mother and sisters. Sitting in the center of the arrangement was a white, stuffed bear who was later named Shaky because of the rattle inside her that shook whenever she was handled. The bear became my daughter's dearest stuffed companion, playing with her all day long and then snuggling close to her every night.

But after three years of constant use, Shaky started looking a little rough. Her stuffing had compressed and then shifted out of her neck so that it offered little or no support to her head, which flopped around haphazardly whenever my daughter handled her. Her ears were almost threadbare and had migrated from pure white to sea-foam green.

My daughter was unaware of the changes, but my wife and I watched Shaky's deterioration with dismay and alarm. Any parent can tell you about the horror of their child losing a beloved stuffed animal and the grief and chaos that follow. We were looking at the day when Shaky would melt in the washing machine and no amount of thread would be able to put her back together.

So we came up with a plan. We researched and found an exact duplicate of Shaky online. I don't remember whether we even looked at the price. It didn't really matter. We had to have a plan in place quickly if disaster was to be averted. We bought the new Shaky and planned to switch her out with the old Shaky without my daughter's knowledge. Then we would retire the old Shaky in a box in the closet so she might have a better chance at longevity. Like all plans, it sounded great until it was executed. Then it started to unravel.

The new Shaky arrived in the mail one afternoon, and I made the switch while my daughter was napping. When she awoke, my wife and I were both there, smiling at her and, well, waiting to see if we had gotten away with making the change.

"Here's Shaky!" we both said with fake smiles plastered on our faces, both of us overacting as if we were the stars of a Jim Carrey movie.

My daughter looked at us and then looked at the new Shaky. "Is this Shaky?" she asked with doubt in her eyes.

My wife and I looked at each other and then at my daughter. We had intended to enact a temporary deception for my daughter's own good, but we hadn't counted on having to tell her an outright lie.

"Uh, here's Shaky!" we repeated, hoping she wouldn't press the issue.

I'm proud to say we kept our composure and continued to smile at my daughter, but my wife told me later she could see a bead of sweat making its way down my temple. We both were stalling, watching each other to see which direction the other would go. Do we tell her an out-and-out lie, or do we come clean? We had never lied to her before and didn't want to start now, but if we fessed up, the whole plan would be blown. So we continued to stall, answering our daughter with indirect, nonsensical answers like the ones politicians use when they're cornered.

"This doesn't look like Shaky. Is this Shaky?" my daughter asked.

"Um, what do you think about Shaky? Isn't Shaky pretty?" we answered.

"Is this Shaky?" my daughter pressed.

"Uh, say 'hi' to Shaky!"

My daughter looked at us as if we had lost our minds.

Finally, we gave up our ruse and told her about our strategy to save the original Shaky. She was very dubious at first and took a lot of convincing, but in time, she came to see the merits of semiretiring Shaky.

Some people might think we were nuts to hesitate in deceiving our daughter for her own good, but we were thinking about the long game. Over the years, we have tried to give our kids a consistent, unwavering foundation of honesty so they know that when we tell them something, they can count on it being the truth. That doesn't mean we tell them everything or that they have the right to know everything. They don't. We tell them only the things that are relevant to their lives and are age-appropriate. Our hope is that we are building in them an internal foundation of trust—that they will know they can rely on what we tell them about who they are, who God is, and how the world works.

As for the Shaky saga, the new bear was given a name of her own—Faithful. And Faithful stepped in to relieve many of the day-to-day responsibilities of Shaky, who now sits in a place of honor on my daughter's shelf. Occasionally, though, Shaky is pulled off the shelf and is lovingly cuddled while my daughter sleeps, because after all, there is only one Shaky.

The Takeaway

Teach your kids to have integrity by setting an example of honesty in your home at all times.

16

Little People Are Watching

Our day of family fun had finally arrived. My wife had planned a family outing at the Georgia Aquarium, and the kids were literally hopping with excitement.

To be perfectly honest, I had mixed feeling about going for a couple of reasons. First, it's a little hard for me to switch gears from take-care-of-my-family mode to goof-off-for-the-whole-day mode. And second, I hate to admit it, but contrary to countless theme-park advertisements, it sometimes seems there's no such thing as "fun for the whole family." It's just a fact of life that what kids want to do can often bore the daylights out of parents, and what parents think is interesting is liquid boredom to the kids. To paraphrase Jerry Seinfeld, there never will be fun for the whole family until they install a gun range and nail salon at Chuck E. Cheese.

Nevertheless, the big day had come, and I was doing my best to enter into the moment and enjoy some time off with my wife and kids. So on a cool November morning, we drove from the outer suburbs of Atlanta all the way downtown. We navigated our way to the aquarium parking deck and found a great space close to the elevator. As everyone was piling out of the car, I heard a dull thunk from the passenger side.

I ran around to the other side of the car, where my wife was looking down at the door of the car beside us with a worried expression on her face. She had just put a sizable ding into a brand-new 700 Series BMW beside our car. Man, it hurts to even write those words.

I wanted to pretend it hadn't happened and keep walking to the aquarium. But the problem with that was twofold.

First, I believe that when the Lord told us to "do unto others..." he didn't mean to treat people right only when it's convenient for us, but to make a point of doing it day in and day out. I'll be the first one to tell you that I don't always get it right in this area, but there are times when it's a hard principle for me to ignore (as much as I really would like to), and this was one of those times.

The second problem was that little people were watching to see what their dad would do. At that particular moment, I wasn't feeling especially spiritual. I was mad at the situation. I was mad at my wife for placing me in that situation, and frankly, I wanted to let her have an earful.

But then I saw something right in front of me that I couldn't ignore. I knew for certain that either way, no matter what I chose to do, my kids were going to remember this day. I knew that they were either going to remember a great family day when we all got to see some awesome sea creatures, or they were going to remember Dad having a fit because he was upset. The funny thing is, they might not even remember why Dad got upset—just that he blew up and the day was ruined for everyone.

So I took a moment. I told everyone I needed to be alone for a minute, and I walked away and grumbled to myself. I might have even prayed that the Lord would help me through this situation. Then I walked back to my family and wrote a note apologizing for the damage, listing my name and number. I hated writing every word of that note because each one made me feel like I was spending a hundred dollars.

But little people were watching. They needed to see their dad do the right thing with the ding. They needed to see their dad let their mom off the hook and tell her that he understands, that the shoe could have easily been on the other foot. They needed to see Dad practice what he preaches.

I don't always get it right. Sometimes I blow it. In those times, I need to make it right because little people are watching. Little people are always watching.

The Takeaway

Prepare your children for the character challenges they will face by setting a good example.

17

Mother's Day Surprise

Alison wasn't surprised when she didn't get anything for Mother's Day. That was the way it had been since she was married. Her husband, Tim, told her that he just wasn't the present-giving type, that he loved her, but all that gift-giving stuff just wasn't him. The first and last time she had received a gift from Tim had been on the Christmas before they were married, when he gave her a diamond engagement ring. Since then, 17 years had passed without one gift, one card, one remembrance of any special day.

It wasn't that she was materialistic. She would have been happy with a card, some flowers picked from the yard, or anything, really. But occasion after occasion, year after year, Tim showed not the slightest interest in celebrating any special day.

She told herself that such things aren't important in a marriage, that love is built on commitment and trust, not birthdays and anniversaries. So Alison buried her hurt feelings and tried to understand. Even so, she couldn't help getting a little excited when special days rolled around. Maybe this was the year Tim would make an effort. After all, she had always made a big deal out of his special days. Every year she and their two kids surprised Tim on his birthday with presents and a cake. Each Christmas Alison made sure there were presents for him under the tree. Every Father's Day she and the kids gave Tim cards and gifts. Every anniversary and Valentine's Day she was sure to get Tim at least a card. Somewhere in the back of her mind, she hoped Tim would want to reciprocate all the blessings he had received. Whenever she had tried to hint that it might be nice to have something from him, he would reply with something like, "That's how I am. Quit trying to change me!"

It made everything worse that their kids had followed Tim's example. Without even thinking about it, Tim had taught their children that "normal" in their household was that Dad is celebrated with affirmation and gifts, but those things don't really apply to Mom. Both of their kids were under ten years old, so they took the arrangement at face value and didn't give it much thought.

So Alison didn't expect to get anything for Mother's Day. She certainly didn't expect what Tim wound up giving her. During the heat of an argument, Tim blurted out that he had been seeing another woman. He blamed Alison for his affair—if she had been more attentive, if she had been a better wife, if she had taken care of his needs, then he wouldn't have had to go looking for love in the arms of another woman.

Alison was completely taken by surprise. She had known their marriage was far from ideal but had no idea that she would awaken to this kind of surprise on Mother's Day. But Tim's Mother's Day surprises were far from over. While Alison was in the bedroom dealing with the tragic news she had just received, Tim called his kids into the kitchen for a family conference.

"Kids, I don't love your mom anymore," he said, "so you're getting a new mommy. I already have her picked out for you."

Happy Mother's Day, right?

There are so many things that I hate about this tale. I hate Tim's disrespect, his unfaithfulness, and his attitude. But one of the things I hate most is that Tim's kids will most likely grow up to repeat this behavior because it was modeled for them in their own home. His daughter will learn that she doesn't deserve respect or affirmation from the men in her life. She will most likely seek attention from guys who disrespect or abuse her. His son will learn to take the women in his life for granted—to believe that women are superfluous, existing only to serve him.

What are you teaching your kids about relationships? Do you celebrate the woman in your life? Do you take the time? Do you make an effort? Your gesture doesn't have to be perfect. It doesn't need to be grandiose. It only needs to be heartfelt and sincere.

And celebrating your wife isn't only for birthdays and anniversaries. It's about how you treat her on a daily basis. Every day, through your actions and inactions, you are programming your children for either success or failure in their future relationships.

The Takeaway

Prepare your children for marriage by making every effort to celebrate your wife and treat her with respect.

18

Seven Powers Empowerment

One of the main reasons I began writing motivational books was to communicate the success principles that nobody told me about when I was growing up.

It's not that I didn't receive instruction. In school I was taught history, math, science, and grammar. At church I learned about God, the Bible, and spiritual things. I took private lessons to learn music and how to play an instrument or two. My dad and big brother taught me a bit about sports. But not once do I remember anyone sitting down with me and saying, "Okay, Charles, whatever you decide to do with your life, you are going to need to understand how success works." Maybe that was because I was too thickheaded to be told anything, but still I can't help thinking now that I could have saved myself an immense amount of time and trouble if I had been taught these simple principles.

Instead, I labored for years under the notion of fairy-tale thinking, the belief that success would magically come to me someday if I behaved myself and waited patiently, like Cinderella on prom night. After I wandered down that disappointing and bitter road for a few years, it slowly dawned on me that if I were to see any success in my life, I would have to do something about it.

I began practicing a different life philosophy and started seeing dramatic changes in my life in every area. I eventually espoused these principles in a book and titled it *The Seven Powers of Success*.

I believe that if kids are to see any success in their future at all—whether physical, emotional, relational, financial, or spiritual—it is imperative that we teach them these principles. To that end, my kids' summer job last year was to read *The Seven Powers of Success.* For each chapter they read, they were to write a one-page report demonstrating they had a firm handle on the principles discussed in that chapter.

My message to them was clear: It pays to arm yourself with knowledge, to seek wisdom, and prepare yourself for life's challenges. Once they worked their way through *The Seven Powers of Success,* I paid them to read and give me book reports on my first book, *Shattering the Glass Slipper.* Now, I daresay that either one of them can articulate the principles in those books almost as well as I can.

It's not my intention to comprehensively cover the Seven Powers here, because I think I already did a pretty good job of spelling them out in the book that bears their name. But I figure that if I'm writing a book about becoming a better dad, I'd be negligent to not at least briefly describe them, so here they are.

The Power of Choice. Your kids need to know that they are responsible for the direction of their lives. They need to know that entitlement robs them of any sense of accomplishment. No one else has the power to control their destiny.

The Power of Vision. How many times are kids encouraged to look into their future in a realistic way? Instead of simply asking a child what she wants to be when she grows up, why not have a dialogue with her about what she wants her life to look like, where she wants to wind up, what her motives are, and what she must do to create that reality?

The Power of Mind. It's the difference between knowledge and wisdom—between owning a tool and knowing how to use it. We send our kids to school to gain knowledge, but how much time do we spend encouraging them to seek wisdom? It is not what a person knows, but how he uses that knowledge that determines his level of success in any endeavor.

The Power of Action. Success favors the audacious. Unless we teach our kids to act, to initiate, and to engage, they are destined for a life of mediocrity. Most people in the world are content to watch others step up, but the notable exceptions are the ones who get an idea and put it into motion.

The Power of Failure. What lessons do your kids take away from their failures? What do they do with that failure after the tears, frustration, and humiliation? What lesson will they learn from your own behavior when you fall on your face? Do your kids see failure as something to be ashamed of or as an instructor leading them to greater challenges and achievement?

The Power of Character. None of us is perfect, but it is a fact that your children are learning character by observing your every action. Mind you, they're picking it up from other places as well, such as the media and their community, but make no mistake—you are the first brick in the foundation of their character.

The Power of Belief. Do you intentionally instill in your children a belief in themselves that is founded on achievement and their innate ability? Do you train your kids to invest in the lives of the people around them? And do you help them develop a positive and healthy worldview?

If you trust that your kids will accidentally acquire and apply these seven traits, you are sadly mistaken. The principles of success are not intuitive. They contrast with human inclination. In a world that is actively attempting to lure your children into entitlement and enslavement, your kids are depending on you to give them the gift of empowerment.

The Takeaway

Give your children their best shot at success by teaching them to harness, develop, and apply their Seven Powers.

19

Guiding with Grace

For all intents and purposes, Dan was an only child. He arrived late in the Timmerson family, so all of his siblings were grown and out of the house by the time Dan came along. I moved in a couple houses down the street from Dan, and we soon started hanging out with each other, riding our bikes, playing army, wandering through the woods, and whatever else ten-year-old boys did for entertainment before the days of video games and the Internet.

Dan's father was an ex-preacher who worked around town as a master carpenter. Dan was extremely proud of his father and lost no opportunity to tell me and any other neighborhood kids who would listen just what a great carpenter his dad was. To hear Dan tell it, there wasn't any cabinet or piece of furniture that Mr. Timmerson couldn't build. His father had a real wood shop in a shed behind his house with a professional-grade table saw, drill press, grinding stone, and about a half dozen other things that looked like they could kill or disable me if I ever dared to touch them. Even so, Dan and I used to sneak into the shop and check out all his dad's cool tools when he was at work. Dan's dad had taught him how to use some of the power tools, and he was allowed to use a few of them even when his father wasn't around.

One day, I went over to Dan's house and found him hard at work on a project. The Timmersons were one of the only neighborhood families that owned a riding lawn mower, and Dan was building a trailer for it that could be used to haul trash, limbs, and weeds. I stood around and watched Dan measure the wood with care and cut it with precision. After that, he sanded all the wood and joined the pieces together with shiny new bolts and screws. Then, after the whole thing was assembled, he took some sandpaper and went over it again, touching it up. He worked furiously all day long and envisioned the moment his father would come home, see it, and say a word or two in praise.

Dan finished the job just minutes before his father arrived. It was a remarkable accomplishment that any kid could be proud of. The new wooden trailer was about three by four feet and was mounted atop a metal frame with wheels that Dan had salvaged. I'm not sure I could replicate the quality of that trailer even now if I were put to the test.

As soon as his father pulled into the driveway, Dan was calling to him. "Dad! Dad! Come to the backyard—I made something I want to show you!"

His father sauntered to the backyard and inspected the new trailer with the critical eye of a master carpenter. In great detail, he pointed out the errors in construction and design of the project. The wood was mismatched. The frame of the trailer should have been placed on the outside rather than the inside so that the sticks and yard trash didn't get caught inside the trailer when it was dumped out. The corners should have been reinforced for extra strength. Everything he said was technically correct yet not at all what his son needed. I still remember Dan's face falling with each word his father spoke. The next day Dan took a crowbar and, with tears in his eyes, dismantled the whole thing, piece by piece. He never rebuilt it.

I don't want to sound like I'm coming down too hard on Dan's dad. Maybe things weren't going his way. Maybe he had trouble at work. Maybe he had money problems. Even in the best of times, it's not easy for a parent to switch from work mode to family mode. It's hard to always be on point when your kids need something from you. I know that sometimes my kids can catch me in a bad moment and I don't react well.

The real challenge in parenting is to wield the tools of instruction with one hand while fanning the flame of encouragement with the other—to teach while inspiring, to correct and yet praise. To do the one and neglect the other will always produce dysfunction. The next time you need to give constructive criticism to your kids, try a formula that I heard from Pastor Joe Chamber in Everett, Washington:

RL x 3 + NT x 1.

The RL stands for "really like," and you have to use it three times before you get to use the rest of the formula.

"Dan, I *really like* how you repurposed some of the scrap wood we have lying around here. I also *really like* that you found a useful, constructive way to use your time. I also *really like* the craftsmanship you put into this project. I can tell you really worked hard on it."

Then you're ready for the NT, or the "next time" part of the formula.

"Here's an idea for you, Dan. Next time, try stabilizing the corners with some L-brackets. That'll make it more steady and it will last longer."

See the difference? Who wouldn't respond better to guidance with grace? The crucial thing for us dads to remember is that our objective is not to build great trailers, but to build awesome young people.

The Takeaway

Train your kids to be able to receive instruction and hear valuable input given to them by authority figures.

20

What's in a Name?

Several years ago when Quaker State went into the quick oil-change business, they had a radio ad campaign that I thought was particularly clever. The ads started with a brief story that ended with a punch line, and they closed with their slogan.

I can't remember any of the specific ads, but they typically went something like this:

> Ever since he was a little boy, Sal dreamed of opening his own restaurant. As he grew, Sal constantly imagined the savory dishes he would serve and spent every day practicing cooking and planning the menu for the restaurant he would one day own. For years and years Sal worked odd jobs around his village, saving every penny he earned for that glorious day when he could afford to own a business. The day he opened the doors of the eatery bearing his own name was the proudest day of his life. High above the doors hung the name of his new establishment: the Sal Monella Restaurant.
>
> He was out of business in a week.
>
> What's in a name? Everything.

The really odd thing about those commercials is that the Quaker State quick oil-change places are pretty much extinct now, but I think their ads made a great point: A name can lead to greatness or disaster.

The naming of our children was of great importance to my wife and me, and we prayed about what to name our kids before we were even expecting. By the time we found out we were pregnant with our first child, we had no doubt that we were to name her Faith Christina.

Since our faith has always been a part of our lives, we wanted to give her a name that reflected that value and our commitment to God.

When our son came along, we also prayed about what to name him and felt we were to name him Charles Wesley, not only because it's my name but also because it was my grandfather's. The name Charles means "strong and manly," and Wesley means "from the west meadow," implying prosperity.

Just about every name means something, and the great majority mean something good. When you give a child a name, you give them a target, something to live up to. Most people walk around directionless, not knowing their purpose or the meaning of their lives. While a name can't completely answer those questions for your children, it can certainly help point them in the right direction. It helps set their vision and identify where they want to be.

My wife and I often remind our kids what their names mean, especially when they're having a tough time. If my son is struggling in some area, I will remind him that his name means "strength" and that I know he will overcome his obstacle. When my daughter is having a challenge, I remind her of her name's meaning and that it's important that we trust God.

We think about preparing our kids for the road ahead in almost every area—financially, spiritually, physically, and emotionally. But I believe it's also important that we prepare a vision. I don't mean that we should tell them what vocation they need to pursue or whom they need to marry, but simply that we need to give them some sense of destiny—a destiny they can build themselves.

What's in a name? A roadmap, a challenge, a promise, a destiny, encouragement, hope, and connection. It is a gift you give to your child that will guide them throughout their entire lives.

The Takeaway

Use your children's names as tools to prepare them to face the world with a firm grasp on who they are. Implant a strong identity within them to which they can aspire.

21

Sorry About That

When you're young, few people in the world can make you as mad as your siblings. They seem to know when you are most vulnerable and precisely where to poke you to elicit the biggest reaction. The fights are inevitable.

I can't begin to count the times my sisters and I had it out—explosive, screaming, end-of-life-as-we-know-it fights, sometimes one on the heels of the other. It must have driven my parents half crazy. It's a wonder they didn't hop a train out of town in the dead of night.

But they endured our squabbles, and more important, they made sure we resolved our differences. We didn't have to agree with each other. We didn't have to feel repentant. We didn't even have to like each other. But one thing my parents insisted on was that we apologize to each other. We had to look one another in the eye and say the words "I'm sorry."

Relationships often fail for lack of these two little words. Whether relationships are personal or professional, familial or financial, without these two words, they are almost guaranteed to implode. These are the hardest two words for anyone to utter, especially when the blood is boiling, feelings are hurt, and resentment is high.

It's amazing that we talk so little about these words in our society. We come close. We dance all around them. We hear sermons about the importance of forgiving one another. We read books about how important it is to not harbor resentment toward another person. But when was the last time you heard anyone talk about apologizing? When was the last time you read a book about your obligation to humble yourself and go man up, fess up, and own up? Better still, when was the last time you heard anyone suggest that parents apologize to their kids?

Almost everyone I've ever asked has told me their parents never apologized to them. Not once. I wonder why that is. Is it because the parents feel that by doing so, they will undermine their authority? Or is it because they think apologizing makes them appear weak? Or is it just good old pride? They don't apologize because the thick wall of their own pride is too strong for them to break through.

Whatever the reason, not upholding the discipline of apologizing in your household is damaging your kids' future relationships. If they don't know how to resolve differences by the time they say "I do," their marriages are going to be exponentially more difficult. And by apologize, I mean these three things.

1. Recognize that in every conflict, each party has done or said something wrong. Take ownership of whatever wrongs you committed before or during the altercation, and confess your wrongs to the offended party.

2. Look the offended person in the eye and say the words, "I'm sorry that I (state what you did wrong)." It's important that you list your offenses specifically. If you can't remember what you did or said wrong, I guarantee you the other person can help you remember. It's also important that you make the other person believe you mean it. If you are insincere, your apology will fall flat and be ineffective.

3. Make amends for whatever you did wrong. It's amazing to me how some people can spend two hours in a fight tearing down a relationship and then think that a mumbled apology will magically make everything better. Here's the rule: You have to put as much effort into making things right again as you did in tearing them down. You need to be willing to speak as many words repairing the relationship as the ones you used to rip it up. If you spent an hour telling someone how horrible they are, you owe it to them to spend as much time as it takes before the other party is made whole again.

Unless you do all three of these steps, your apology is incomplete. If you mumble, "I shouldn't have done that" and then walk away, you haven't repaired the relationship. If you throw out a halfhearted,

"Sorry," don't expect anyone to fall over themselves rushing to forgive you. If you don't try to make amends, it's questionable how sorry you really are for your trespasses.

And how are your children supposed to learn these behaviors? The best way is by seeing you practice them. Yes, you will have to give them some instruction and hold them to a standard, but if they see the authority figures in their own household practicing the discipline of genuine apology, they will adopt that standard and carry it with them into future relationships. You are giving them the gift of less strife and more harmony. And what parent wouldn't want that for their child? And all it will cost you is your pride, which you didn't need to be carrying around anyway.

The Takeaway

Prepare your children to have successful relationships by teaching them the value and power of saying, "I'm sorry."

Part 4

PROTECT

He will command his angels concerning you
to guard you in all your ways;
they will lift you up in their hands,
so that you will not strike your foot against a stone.

PSALM 91:11-12

Good Dads Hold On

Edie and Rusty Howard were finishing dinner with their kids at a local restaurant early one Sunday evening in May 2011. Their young family included a five-year-old daughter named Harli and 19-month-old son named Hayze. Edie had to go back to work at Freeman Hospital, so they agreed that Rusty would take the kids home with him in his truck while Edie drove herself to work in the car.

Edie kissed the kids good-bye, and then Rusty loaded them into his truck and started driving back home. As Edie drove to the hospital, fierce winds began rocking her car.

She didn't realize it at that time, but she was driving in one of the worst tornadoes in the country's history. Had the tornado been trying to tear a path straight through the heart of Joplin, Missouri, it couldn't have done a better job. The monster tornado was as big and terrible as they come—up to a mile wide with winds in excess of 200 miles per hour.

The damage was catastrophic. Almost 7000 homes were utterly destroyed. Many public buildings, such as churches, schools, and fire stations were completely leveled. Entire businesses and neighborhoods were turned into kindling in only a matter of minutes. In the end, 158 people lost their lives.

Edie Howard was so worried about the violent winds assaulting her car that she called Rusty, who told her he would seek cover in the nearby Home Depot. Rusty pulled into the store parking lot, grabbed his children out of the truck, and hurried into the store. Moments after entering the store, it was demolished by the tornado, killing Rusty, Harli, and Hayze.

Their obituary in the *Joplin Globe* reads, "Harli and Hayze were found securely in their daddy's arms."

Because that's what good dads do.

Good dads always hold on.

Almost every dad I know would make the same decision and do the same thing Rusty did. Because it's the right thing to do. It's a dad's job to hold on no matter what. Most dads know this, but others are still trying to grasp this point.

I remember talking with a gentleman named Peter after I spoke at his church in Kentucky. When I asked about his family, he told me he had a couple kids who live in Minneapolis. I asked him when he had last seen them, and he answered that it had been five or six years. Things had gotten tough with the kids' mom, and she had moved away. She had made it clear to him that life would be better for all of them if he weren't involved, so she took off and he let go.

I had heard stories like Peter's a dozen times before, so his wasn't new to me, but it was still heartbreaking to hear. At that time both of my kids were under five years old, and I couldn't imagine not seeing them grow up.

"How can you stand to not see your kids?" I asked Peter.

"Oh, I don't know," he answered. "You just get used to it, I guess."

I don't know Peter. I don't know what his inner motivations were or exactly what was going on in his head when he made that decision (or when he allowed that decision to be made for him). But I remember thinking that maybe there are some things we're not supposed to get used to. Maybe not ever seeing your children again is one of them.

Children need their dads to hold on to them. They're counting on them to say, "Nothing in heaven or on earth will keep me from you. When life hurts most, I will wrap my arms around you and do everything in my power to hold on. The winds may blow, the earth might tremble, and everything around you may come crashing down, but whatever happens, I will be right beside you, holding on."

What would happen if a child grew up believing that? What would happen if dads clung to their kids with the tenacity and courage of someone like Rusty Howard?

What usually happens is security. The child's core programming translates that voice into self-worth and value, which are manifested in a quiet confidence that the world will challenge but can never steal.

The Takeaway

Good dads weather the storms of life and protect the bond between themselves and their children.

23

The Dad Deal

A number of years ago, I spoke at a church about the Father-heart of God and told a few of my stories about being a dad. After the service, I was standing at the back of the church as guest speakers do, greeting people and selling a few of my books. The crowd had responded well that morning, and several people came by to tell me they appreciated what I had to say. I was getting ready to close up shop and head home when a middle-aged man approached me and offered his hand for me to shake. He smiled and said, "Hey, I really related to what you were talking about this morning. I'm a dad too."

He told me his name was Gary. Then he gestured to a teenage girl standing beside him and said, "This is my daughter, Casey." Casey smiled at me and said hello, looking both blessed that her dad was making such a big deal out of her and embarrassed that her parent was talking to her in public.

"Mind if I tell you a quick story?" Gary asked.

"I'd love to hear it," I replied.

Gary put his arm around his daughter and said, "Casey almost wasn't here today." He smiled lovingly at his daughter and she grinned back at him. This was obviously a story she had heard before.

"How do you mean?" I asked.

Gary looked thoughtful for a moment and then said, "A number of years ago, just before Casey reached her third birthday, we were outside our home in the front yard. She was running around playing while I was raking some leaves. I took my eyes off her for just a second, and she was gone."

I told Gary I could relate to that. It's hard watching the kids when you're a dad. I've noticed you can watch them all day long and they don't move, but then you take your eyes off them for only three or four hours, and they're gone. What's a guy to do?

"I immediately started looking for her," Gary continued. "After only about a minute or two, I spotted her. She was standing in the road waving at me, saying, 'Hey, Daddy! Hey, Daddy! I'm over here!'

"What I saw next made my blood run cold. As she was waving at me with a big smile on her face, a large, three-axle delivery truck was heading down the street right toward her. I could tell from the speed and direction of the truck that the driver hadn't seen her."

Gary paused for a moment and closed his eyes as he relived his nightmare. "I don't remember thinking anything at that point," he said. "I don't remember making a decision or coming up with a plan.

"All I remember is moving. I ran as fast as I could and watched in horror as the truck sped toward my little girl. I was almost to her when I realized I wasn't going to make it, so I dove toward her and managed to shove her out of the way."

Gary exchanged another smile with his daughter. "As you can see," he continued, "she came out of the situation with hardly any injury at all. I almost made it too," he said, as he picked up a cane that I hadn't noticed before. "Now I have to use this thing, but I'm a lot better off now than I was just after the accident."

"What happened then?" I prodded.

He shrugged and said, "Most of my body cleared the truck, but my right leg got run over by the wheels on the far side of the vehicle."

He lifted his leg onto a nearby chair and pulled up his pant leg. Scar tissue crisscrossed his leg like lines on a Rand McNally road map. Just looking at it was painful. I couldn't imagine what experiencing it had been like.

"Every square inch of bone below the knee was crushed." He pointed to several round scars that dotted his leg, saying, "These are where the screws were for the pins they put in my leg afterward."

"Does it still hurt?" I asked.

"Oh, most of the time it's not too bad. It always starts aching whenever it's going to rain." He chuckled softly, and said, "The good news is that I'm always the first one around here who knows what the weather's going to be!"

The thing that strikes me as I recall my conversation with Gary is that he was smiling most of the time he was relating his tale. He wasn't smiling because he knew he had done something awesome. He wasn't a macho, tough guy bragging about an incredibly brave thing he had done. He was just an ordinary-looking, middle-aged guy telling me a story about his daughter.

I think the reason he was smiling was that he felt he had made a good deal. One precious, irreplaceable daughter at the cost of one leg. And I got the feeling Gary would make the same decision today if he had to. Most of the dads I know feel the same way.

As I listened to Gary's story, I related to it on two levels—as a father and as a son.

Since I became a father, for the first time in my life, I know what it feels like to be willing to jump in front of danger for another human being.

As a son, it reminded me of what God did for me. Just like that little girl (but nowhere nearly as innocent), I was standing in life's road, living life as I saw fit, not caring a bit about the dangerous consequences my actions would bring. There was a giant delivery truck heading toward me, but I was too foolish to get out of the way. But then a hand came from 2000 years in the past and pushed me out of danger's way, and I escaped injury. But the hand that saved me didn't escape. That hand was pierced and mangled on my account.

Sometimes I can imagine Jesus pointing to his scars in heaven, saying, "That scar bought me Charles. This one bought me Diane. This one bought Carol. This one, Reggie."

That's how love works. It's willing to sacrifice itself for the betterment of others.

Most of us dads won't ever have to literally throw ourselves in front of a moving truck. But most of us will be called upon to sacrifice our finances, dreams, well-being, time, or talent for our kids. And that's okay because of what it buys us. When the time comes, we'll make that deal, and we'll smile about it later.

The Takeaway

A father will gladly sacrifice anything he possesses—up to and including his own life—in order to protect his children and purchase their lives.

24

Standing Guard and Protecting Innocence

When I attended college in the early 1980s, I had the chance to meet many students from faraway lands, such as Egypt, Colombia, Guatemala, Ecuador, and Brazil. They had come to Hattiesburg, Mississippi, to attend the University of Southern Mississippi English Language Institute. I had the pleasure of getting to know quite a few of these students, and some of them became my good friends.

Late one Friday night, I was hanging out in my apartment with one such friend as he spoke to me about his homeland with great passion and pride. It had been three long years since Alberto had been home, and he was understandably homesick. His eyes lit up with excitement as he described the people, music, language, and scenery of the country he had left so that he could pursue an education in the United States.

He also desperately missed his mother and sister, whom he had not seen since he had left his country. They wrote often and spoke on the phone when they could, but in the days before smartphones, email, and texts, the distance between family members was sorely felt. When I asked about his father, Alberto's mood darkened abruptly. "I don't ever talk with him," he mumbled.

I ventured to dig a bit deeper and asked, "Do you mind if I ask why that is?"

"Because he's evil," Alberto snapped. After we talked a bit more, Alberto opened up and told me that his father had never been much of a presence in his life. His childhood memories were punctuated with intermittent appearances of a loud, foul, abusive man who was drunk most of the time. He would show up at their home out of the blue, create chaos in their family for a few weeks, spend all their money, and then disappear again for months at a time.

On Alberto's fifteenth birthday, his father appeared and announced that he was taking Alberto for a ride. Alberto was excited because his father had never shown the slightest interest in his birthday, much less arranged for a birthday excursion. But for some reason, his mother was extremely upset by the idea and argued vehemently with his father about the plan. His father prevailed as always, so Alberto and his dad headed out the door.

As they drove away from his home, his father smirked and told Alberto that he was giving him a great present on this day. He said that today Alberto would become a man. Alberto couldn't begin to imagine what his father meant and was surprised when they drove to the seediest part of town and parked in front of the town brothel.

Because young people read my books, I'll refrain from detailing what followed. Suffice to say, what his father intended as a gift, Alberto perceived as a curse.

There in my small apartment in Hattiesburg, my friend openly wept as he recalled the horror of the experience. It was the worst day of his life. He felt humiliated, violated, abused, and confused. With tears streaming down his cheeks, Alberto asked me why his father, of all people, would expose him to such a thing. Wasn't it a father's job to protect and lead? Although he was just a boy, Alberto intuitively knew that a sacred trust had been broken. Instead of protecting his innocence, his father had intentionally exposed him to the basest kind of carnality.

Every child comes into this world with a special gift of innocence, and it is up to the parent to guard that innocence at all costs. Innocence is a fragile flower—once crushed, it can never be restored. Once you have eaten from the tree of the knowledge of good and evil, you can never return to your state of innocence. You can't un-learn. You can't un-know. You can't un-see. You have changed.

Alberto's story is an extreme example of neglecting to protect a child's innocence, but how often do we allow movies, TV, video games, and the Internet to incrementally violate our kids' innocence? Why would we assume that it is any more healthy for them to be exposed to sexual (or violent, for that matter) materials through media than in real life? Why would we think that since it is so common, it must be okay?

There is a time for young people to come into such delicate and privileged knowledge. It is up to parents to walk *with* their children into that knowledge and provide guidance along the way. As fathers, that means we stand guard and watch over our little flocks. We make sure that our little ones (girls and boys) don't have their innocence ripped away from them.

No, you can't cover all the bases all the time, and sometimes the enemy steals a base on you. But if you can maintain vigilance, you can get it mostly right and give your kids a better chance of avoiding the pain and dysfunction that plagues so much of our society.

The Takeaway

A father must do all that is within his power to protect the innocence of his children.

25

The Film Fear Factor

It seems so corny now. Laughable really. But when I watched *Earth vs. the Flying Saucers* on TV when I was nine years old, it flat-out scared the living bejeebers out of me. Most of the movie wasn't all that bad. I could handle the flying saucers zipping around the sky. I was okay with the battle with the aliens on the military base. But the part that really got me was when the group of earth people entered the saucer. When that glowing, flower-shaped communication device slowly descended from the ceiling and (spoiler alert!) drained the brains of the general and policeman, for some reason that did me in. I remember being afraid to look around corners for days afterward for fear of aliens jumping out of the shadows and sucking my brains out. Not that I would have lost too much. If my grades back then were any indication, it might have even added a couple points to my IQ.

I had the same experience when I first saw the Wicked Witch of the West's flying monkeys on *The Wizard of Oz*. Man-a-livin', that's scary cinema. Again, the witch herself wasn't that bad, but you throw some wings on a few dozen monkeys, and you have yourself a real horror flick.

When I was a little older, I watched a Dracula movie that shook me up so much that I was afraid to go to sleep afterward. I finally gave up around four a.m. and said to all the hidden vampires in my room, "Okay, if you're going to get me, go ahead. I've got to get some sleep."

It's amazing how terrified I was watching all of those goofy movies with such weak special effects, but I can assure you—weak or not, those effects did the trick. The fear I felt was real enough.

And all of that is nothing compared to the stuff in movies these days.

I can't tell you how many times I've seen adults walking into PG-13 or R-rated movies with their three- or four-year-old kids. People defend this kind of action by saying things like, "Oh, it doesn't bother my kids! They love it!" But I wonder if it might be closer to the truth to say they haven't *noticed* it bothering their kids. There is a big difference between something not existing and you not noticing its existence. Just because you don't notice a snake in the grass at your feet doesn't mean it can't bite you.

Yes, there comes a day when a child is capable of handling scarier images, but why do we need to place them directly in the path of fear?

The effect of fear in a person can be profound. It is a subtle, hidden force that can bend your perspective and weaken your will. Fear isn't the opposite of faith. It's inverted faith. The mechanism of believing is still at work when you fear. It's just focused on the worst instead of the best. It bends our perspective and shades the way we view the world.

Do we want to build a confident, faith-filled worldview in our kids, or do we want to plant seeds of horror and fear? Kids are naturally going to be afraid at times even without seeing scary films, so why would we unnecessarily populate their subconscious with frightening images?

It's a dad's job to protect his kids from a world that would rob their innocence. That means we need to be aware of what they are visually ingesting. And sometimes it even means getting a sitter the next time we go to the movies.

The Takeaway

Don't allow modern media to implant the seeds of fear in your children.

26

The Fatherhood Standard

In late May, the Kimball family arrived on the gulf coast for their yearly vacation. The kids couldn't wait to get into the ocean, so as soon as the car was parked and the luggage was unloaded, the whole family changed into their swimsuits and ran to the beach.

For the first two days of their vacation, everything went as planned. Dennis and Suzanne had their hands full keeping up with their three active children. The youngest son was still in diapers, so he sat under the beach umbrella, digging in the sand with his shovel and bucket. Their four-year-old girl sat and played on the beach where the waves rolled onto the sand, and their nine-year-old son swam not too far offshore. Dennis and Suzanne swam in the ocean every now and then, but most of the time they relaxed under the beach umbrella, keeping an eye on all the kids.

The third day at the beach began much the same as the first two had. The family had a quick, light breakfast at their rented condo and then headed out to the beach. The kids would have started swimming and playing right away, but their mom insisted that they all stay under the beach umbrella until each one had been thoroughly coated in sunscreen. Afterward, all the kids bolted to their preferred play areas and either swam or dug in the sand to their heart's content.

Somewhere around noon, everyone once again converged at the umbrella for lunch. Sandwiches and potato chips were distributed to the kids, who gobbled them up as if they hadn't seen food for a week. Afterward, Dennis and Suzanne each took a turn walking the kids back to the condo for a bathroom break. A little while later, everyone was back at the beach enjoying a beautiful Florida spring day.

Just after two o'clock, while her attention was on their youngest, Suzanne thought she heard a cry coming from the direction of the ocean. She wasn't immediately concerned because kids always yell when they're having fun. But something about this cry caught her attention, and she stared intently at the spot she last saw her oldest son. After studying the scene for a few seconds, her heart was gripped with fear.

"Dennis," she said, "I can't see Mikey! He was swimming just over there a few minutes ago, and now he's gone!"

Dennis bolted upright and sprinted toward the water. When he got there, he ran a few steps in the surf and then dove headfirst into the waves. Suzanne watched nervously from the water's edge with her youngest son in her arms, her little girl standing by her side. She waited for her husband's head to reappear above the surface of the water, but it never happened. Both he and her oldest son were gone.

Authorities said a rip current had likely led to their demise. People get caught in these strong currents, which pull them away from the shore, and they often drown from fighting the current or from panic. It is a common cause of beach drownings.

Scenes like this are repeated year after year not only at beaches but also at lakes and rivers. And have you noticed that these deaths in water often come in twos? It's not uncommon for someone to plunge in after a child who has disappeared beneath the water. The second person normally goes into the water and gets caught in the same situation as the first, or the first person pulls the would-be rescuer down in desperation.

Often that second person is a dad. It's just what dads do. We protect our kids no matter what. It's expected. It's the standard. It's been that way since the dawn of time and will continue as long as there are dads and kids. That's because at the very center of every dad's heart lies a hero. Someone who is willing to put his children's lives before his own. And what higher calling could a man possibly have than that?

The Takeaway

The greatest call any man could have on his life is to give his life for his children, either figuratively or literally.

27

Not One Word

The entire time I was growing up, I never heard my father say one bad word to my mother. Not once. I never heard him raise his voice to her, complain about her, or insinuate anything negative about her. He never called her a bad name or uttered anything negative about her, either in or out of her presence.

If a disagreement arose between me and my mom, my dad left no doubt as to whose side he would come down on. My mom and dad were a solid, impenetrable unit that you didn't want to mess with. And that's how I grew up thinking a marriage should be.

When I was young, I would repeatedly ask my mom, "Who do you love more? Me or Dad?"

Without question, 100 percent of the time, my mom would tell me that I meant the world to her, but that she loved my father first and foremost. I got the same answer when I asked my father that question.

I didn't grasp my parents' logic at the time, and I was tempted to let my feelings be hurt. It was one of those things they told me I would understand when I got older and had a family of my own. And they were right.

Now I know it's in the family's best interest for the father and mother to love each other first and foremost. Such a bond creates a sense of security in the children and provides stability for the family. If the marital unit isn't strong, the family is at risk.

I've seen it time and time again. A couple falls in love, gets married, and has kids. The to-do list gradually supplants the marriage in importance, and the couple drifts apart. They become coworkers at the job site. The only time they communicate is when they discuss mundane responsibilities. Over time, their exchanges become critical and tense. Other romantic attachments are then made at work, the gym, or the grocery store, and before you know it, either one or the other of the spouses is saying things like, "We just fell out of love. It just wasn't meant to be. God doesn't want me to be unhappy." And *poof*—the marriage disappears, just like that.

How cliché. I never hear anybody talk that way about their car.

"How's that Malibu running?"

"Oh, I don't have that car anymore. I thought it was the one for me, but it started running rough, so the Lord led me to get a new car."

"Man, that's too bad. What was wrong with it?"

"The engine locked up. It turns out the car was deceiving me the whole time. It was really a bad car all along."

"Wait...the engine locked up? Was it out of oil? Did you have a gasket leak?"

"Um, I'm not sure. I never took it to the garage."

"Not even for a tune-up or to have the oil changed?"

"No, you shouldn't have to force a relationship with your car. If it is meant to be, then it'll just work out. It doesn't matter now anyway. God has led me to a new car now."

Do you see how stupid that sounds? What are we teaching our kids about relationships if we allow this form of fairy-tale thinking to dictate the way we manage our relationships? Why not instead make our relationship with our spouse our number one priority? Why not protect our family unit by investing the same amount of effort in keeping our wives as we did in getting them? Isn't that a foundational marketing principle—that getting a customer is harder and more expensive than keeping one you already have? If it's true in the realm of business, why wouldn't it be valid in other relationships?

One simple way to do that is to schedule a regular date night, just the two of you, away from the kids. It's the strangest thing. Every time I'm out with my wife on a date, it reminds me of who we were as a couple before we had kids. It helps us reconnect as a couple rather than as parents. Just about every time we're out on a date, I have a moment when I think, *Wow, I remember this. This is what it feels like to be a couple.*

If you love your kids, put your wife first. Let your kids see you treating her right. Let your words reflect the best in you, not the worst. And let your children feel the security of living in a home guarded by love and protected by a strong marriage.

The Takeaway

Protect your child by not allowing negativity to erode your marriage. Guard your marriage, and you will guard your children's sense of security.

28

Are You Praying to Win?

There was an older couple that attended the same church as my family when I was young. They seemed to be a sweet, loving pair, but one thing always struck me as strange about their relationship. Whenever the conversation turned to any spiritual matter, Mr. Johnson immediately deferred to his wife, saying, "If you want to know about that, you need to ask Helen. She really knows her Bible."

It didn't matter what comment was made or what question was asked. When it regarded God, church, or the Bible, he always had the same response. It wasn't that he didn't have opinions or that he minded sharing them. He had plenty to say about family, business, money, politics, or sports, but when it came to anything of a religious or spiritual nature, his answer was always the same.

"Oh, you should talk to Helen about that. She has a great relationship with the Lord. She's amazing."

Maybe he was just honoring his wife, or maybe he felt she was the better source for such information, but I always thought it odd that as the man of his home, he chose not to show leadership in spiritual matters.

I've seen this lack of leadership in many families. The responsibility for the spiritual well-being of the family should be shared between the father and mother, but often that's not the case. It's often the mom that the kids go to for prayer. It's often the mom that they talk to about their faith questions. It's the mom who prods, exhorts, pleads, and cajoles the family into taking any action regarding their faith. It's great that there are women who are willing to pick up the slack, but what if it's not only the mom's job? What if it's also the father's responsibility to stand at the spiritual gate and defend his family?

I wonder why it is that so many men let the woman of the house shoulder the full load of the family's faith. Maybe these men are mirroring what they saw in their homes when they grew up. Or maybe these men are action-oriented, and the intangible nature of spiritual matters doesn't appeal as much to them. Or maybe to them, the unseen equals the unreal, so it isn't a priority.

Whatever the reason is, men who choose not to lead their families in spiritual matters are missing a great opportunity and neglecting a great responsibility. They're missing the opportunity to demonstrate a man's relevance and importance in the home in a vital area. And they're missing the point that it's their job to go before God to petition for protection for their family.

Dad, have you ever asked yourself who is going to pray for your kids if you don't? Is it really a good idea to let them wander outside your front door without taking a moment to cover them in prayer? The world is a dangerous place, especially for little ones. It seeks to grab their attention, own their values, rob their freedom, steal their innocence, and ultimately, end their lives.

Dad, I know you're busy putting food on the table. I know you're trying to get your family from point A to point B. Please understand that I'm not asking you to be someone you're not. I'm not trying to turn you into a monk who spends 16 hours a day reciting elaborate prayers.

All I'm asking is for you to take a few moments each day to talk to God about your kids. Share your concerns with him and ask for his protection and blessing on your family. It doesn't matter how you do it. You can kneel down or bow your head. You can pray silently or out loud, by yourself or with your family. There is no right or wrong way.

Whatever you do and however you do it, just make sure you get it done. It is far too important of a thing to neglect, because every child deserves to have a praying father.

The Takeaway

Fathers need to recognize the importance of protecting their children by praying for them regularly.

Part 5

PROMOTE

The Son of Man did not come to be served, but to serve, and to give his life as a ransom for many.

MARK 10:45

29

Old Spice and Whiskers

It's difficult for me to separate any memory I have of my father from the smell of Old Spice. For anyone unfamiliar with Old Spice, it is a quality cologne that can be purchased wherever other fine fragrances, such as Aqua Velva or Skin Bracer, are sold. It has a distinct, aptly named aroma that immediately puts one in mind of old men and spices.

In my early twenties, I so closely associated the smell of Old Spice with adulthood and masculinity that I actually bought some and tried wearing it. I remember splashing it on and waiting for the heady rush that only testosterone-laden activities bring. For the first 20 minutes or so of wearing it, I was filled with the same exhilaration I felt when I grew my first chest hair, which also turned out to be my last.

After 30 minutes, though, I noticed the fragrance wasn't fading as colognes often do. It might have even grown a little stronger. I began to long for a breath of fresh air—or any air, really. Then the thought suddenly occurred that I might have jumped the gun by about 30 or 40 years. I clearly wasn't ready for that level of masculinity, so I bolted to the bathroom and washed my face, neck, and hands as thoroughly as I could, but to no avail. The Old Spice had bonded with my DNA and wasn't giving up without a fight. At one point, I feared I was going to have to undergo radiation therapy just to get rid of the smell. Today, 30 years later, I'm proud to say I barely smell of Old Spice at all.

But my dad was man enough to pull it off. He made it work somehow, and I would catch a whiff of it every time I was near him.

My family was affectionate, so when I was a kid, every night I hugged and kissed my dad and mom good night. Eventually I grew up and moved away, but I would still hug and kiss my parents when I visited. My father would crush me into his arms, and I would smell the Old Spice that I so closely associated with him. I would kiss his sandpapery, whiskered cheek and then pull away to see him beaming at me. Both of my parents passed away a number of years ago, and oh, what I would give to have another chance to hug and kiss them once more.

I'm fortunate to have those memories. I know some people who grew up with parents who never hugged or kissed them. Some people have never seen their parents show any affection to each other. Never. Not once.

That's an alien concept to me. My family was far from perfect, but we had affection. Dad would kiss Mom, and all of us kids would yell, "Gross!" while grinning ear to ear. We loved seeing Mom and Dad show affection to one another, and although I didn't know it at the time, it molded and shaped me so that showing affection to my family is a natural thing.

We all need to be touched. We all need to reach out to our loved ones. Without that physical contact, something is missing. Something within us isn't fulfilled.

Today, I hug my son and daughter close to me, and my daughter laughs when I give her what she calls "whiskery kisses." I throw my arms around them when we're walking down the street. We snuggle up next to each other when we're watching a movie. I am constantly patting them on the back or shoulders. I hold my wife's hand, and sometimes when I kiss her, the kids yell, "Gross!" and grin.

And I have my dad and mom to thank for that. They gave me the gift of affection. My dad showed me what it's like to be man enough to wear Old Spice and still be loving with his family. And I'm doing everything I can to pass that gift along to my kids.

The Takeaway

Hugging and kissing are not just for moms! Fathers need to promote love in their homes by hopping on the affection wagon.

Seeing What You Expect

There is an old story of a grandfather sitting on his front porch with his grandson, passing the time of day, watching wagons pass by on the dirt road in front of their home. After a while, a wagon came down the road and stopped in front of their house. Greetings were exchanged, and the man on the wagon told the old man that he was in the process of relocating to the next town down the road. The wagon driver asked the old man what the people were like in the town up ahead.

The old man thought for a moment and replied, "That depends. What were the people like in the town you just came from?"

"They were horrible," the man on the wagon answered. "They were mean and stingy and wouldn't help you if their life depended on it. They all spoke behind your back and never said anything good if they could help it."

The old man answered, "Well, that's pretty much what you're going to find in the town up ahead."

That man rode on, and after a while, another wagon loaded with possessions pulled up to the house.

Once again greetings were exchanged, and the driver of the second wagon told the old man that he, too, was relocating to the next town up the road. He also wanted to know what the people were like there.

"What were the people like in the town you just came from?" the old man asked.

"Nicer people cannot be found," the second driver answered. "Everyone is kind and would give you anything if you needed it."

"Well, I expect that's what you'll find in the town up ahead," the old man said.

After he drove off, his grandson looked up at the old man and said, "Granddad, those two men were going to the same town, right?"

"That's right," the old man said.

"Then why did you tell one of them he would find mean people and the other one he would find nice people?"

The old man smiled and said, "Because most often, you will find the type of people you expect to find. If you believe people are mean, you'll find a way to be disappointed with them. If you believe people are nice, they will be a blessing to you."

All my life people have been telling me how tough the road up ahead is. When my wife and I had our first child, people told me how tough that first year was going to be, and they were right. It was tough, but it was also one of the best years of my life. Then people warned us about "the terrible twos." Our daughter turned two, and she just got better and better. We had the same experience with our son.

Now when people tell me about how tough the teenage years are, I kind of let it go in one ear and out the other. I realize that they are projecting their own perspective and that I don't have to adopt it as my own.

I'm a realist, so I know having kids can be tough. But I'm also a believer, so I know that God can help us overcome any obstacle we encounter in our families if we are open to seeing the best in our kids instead of the worst.

As a father, I am called to champion my kids. To believe in their innate ability to overcome their challenges and be the people God has called them to be. And if we parents don't believe in our own kids, who on earth do you think is going to?

The Takeaway

Promote your kids' confidence by choosing to see the best in them and teaching them to see themselves in a positive light.

31

Exit Stage Right

The reviews of my first play were universally unanimous in their praise of my performance. I don't remember the name of the play since I was only in first grade, but my parents said I really captured the essence of my character, which was listed in the program as Second Tree from the Left. I didn't have any lines, but everyone in my family felt I embodied the full emotion of a tree.

(Warning: If you don't like puns, you probably want to skip the next paragraph.)

Of course, some people said my performance was wooden, that I was going out on a limb taking this role, that it would have been better if I would leaf show business altogether, that I was barking up the wrong tree with acting, that the love of attention would take root in me, and that I would branch out in other forms of entertainment.

(Okay, I've gotten it out of my system. It's safe to continue now.)

My second stage appearance was accidental but just as well received. In second grade, my school had a rule that if the students got too boisterous in the lunchroom, everyone had to remain quiet and not speak one word for the rest of the lunch period. Not speaking has always been a bit of a problem for me, so I started whispering to another kid almost immediately. A teacher caught me and ordered me to eat the rest of my lunch on the cafeteria stage in front of my entire class. Shame was on the menu for that day, and my teacher intended that I get a full helping.

The problem was that I thought it was fantastic. From the stage, I could see the faces of everyone in the room. I looked at the table from which I had just been banished, and I saw the smiling faces of my friends. I smiled back and waved, which elicited a little laugh from them. Then I ate a bite of my sandwich, grabbed my throat, and acted like the school lunch was poisoning me. More kids took notice and started laughing. Then I did a few more food-related improv bits and closed my show with the always-funny Slice of Cheese Hanging on My Nose routine. Classic material. Never fails (with the eight-year-old-and-younger crowd anyway).

By that time my teacher discovered her mistake in placing me on stage as a punishment and came to relieve me of my sentence. I waved again to my friends as I walked off the stage. *Thank you. Thank you. I'll be here all week!*

I sometimes wonder how seminal that incident was in my choosing a performance-based career. I knew at that moment that I loved being on stage and intuitively felt I needed to get back there somehow, someday. In high school, I loved performing in band in both marching and concert seasons. I started performing as a full-time singer/songwriter after high school and then later as a stand-up comedian. Now I get to speak all over the country as a humorous motivational speaker.

But when I became a parent, something changed. I realized that it's one thing to be center stage as a professional speaker, but in my family life, I no longer needed to be in the limelight.

Most of the dads I know (and moms, for that matter) would throw themselves in front of a bus for their kids. They put their kids first and themselves second. But not all parents are like that, are they? Some still think they are the stars of the show, and it's a little sad to see, isn't it?

When I see a parent whose emotional needs come before their child, I wish I could tell them it's much more fulfilling to be in a supporting role, to set the scene so their kids get the applause, recognition, and reward. I wish I could help them see that it's time not to compete for the spotlight but to step back and let their kids shine.

When you are a kid, you are the center of the world, the star of the show. But after you have kids, your job is to be a supporting actor. To tell you the truth, a lot of the time, dads don't even get any speaking lines. Sometimes I just show up and play the part of extra in my kids' movie. And that's okay. It's the way of life.

As a child matures, a parent's job is to gradually move away from being the lead character. First you hold them in your arms. Then you hold their hands as they learn to walk. Then you hold their bicycles when they're learning to ride a bike. Then you learn to let go a bit as you drive them to school, practice, and rehearsals. Then you stand beside them as they get married, and you stand behind them when they have children of their own. Each step they take toward independence means your job is to move off the stage.

The Takeaway

Having children means you are no longer center stage. It is your job to promote and support them as they begin to make their way in the world.

32

It Doesn't Count If You Don't Say It

I've been looking forward to this day for some time now with a mixture of excitement and anxiety. It is a rite of passage that is the responsibility of every dad: teaching his child how to ride a bike. The problem is that I've never actually taught anyone how to ride a bike. I've ridden one myself a thousand times, and I've seen videos of other dads teaching their kids, but I've never had the experience myself. I've never had to put my little girl on a wobbly two-wheel contraption that might throw her onto the pavement at any moment, so I'm a little nervous about how the process will go.

I explain to her that she needs to pedal hard and point the bike straight ahead. I tell her that I will be right beside her, holding the back of the seat to help her balance. She wants my assurance that I'm not going to let go until she's ready, and I tell her I won't. She starts pedaling with all her might while I run alongside her, calling out words of encouragement.

"C'mon, Faith! You can do it! You got this! Keep pedaling, girl! You're awesome! Keep pedaling!"

We repeat this process three or four times, and it occurs to me that I'm not in as good of shape as I used to be. At the end of a run, I'm leaning over with my hands on my knees, huffing and puffing, and my daughter tells me she's ready to try again. We take off once more, and I run alongside her as she concentrates on steering and pedaling. As she picks up speed and is on the verge of going solo, I hear her speaking to herself. "C'mon, Faith! You can do it! You got this! Keep pedaling, girl! You're awesome! Keep pedaling!"

I smile to myself because I realize that not only am I teaching my girl how to ride a bike, I'm teaching her how to talk to herself. I am speaking words of affirmation and encouragement that she has internalized and is now repeating to herself. And I feel like I've given her something of value she can use throughout her life.

Why is it that some people never encourage or affirm their kids? Maybe it's because they never received those gifts from their parents. I've had several people tell me they never heard one word of encouragement from their parents when they were growing up. I can't even imagine how someone could have any chance at success if their parents didn't verbally affirm them.

Words are powerful things. They can build the spirit or break it. They can strengthen character or weaken it. They can elevate or deflate. Words of affirmation are among the best tools you will ever have to build strong, emotionally healthy kids.

How often do you affirm your kids? How many times a day do you say words like these?

"You're an awesome artist."

"You have great character."

"I love to hear you sing."

"You light up the room whenever you walk in."

"I enjoy being with you."

"You really are a good pitcher/catcher/ballplayer."

"I believe in you."

I have no patience with dads who insist their kids know that they think these things about them even though they've never bothered to tell them. It's like knowing your boss values you without him writing you a paycheck. You would know your value a lot better if you were paid, right? Your words are the currency of your love. If your kids know you love and value them, it's because you told them. The words have to be spoken.

On the other side of the equation are the parents who habitually gripe about their kids. Everybody vents about their kids every now and then in an unguarded moment, but I'm talking about the people who constantly talk about just how rotten their kids are. Is it any wonder these kids often find a way to fulfill their parents' poor opinions?

What you say to your kids says more about you than it does about them. Are you a person who takes care to point out the good you see in your kids, or do you find it easier to dwell on the negative? Anybody can point out what's wrong in the world. It takes no special talent or ability. The truly exceptional person is the one who looks for the gold encased within the mountain of stone. And wise is the man who verbally invests in the future of his children.

The Takeaway

Promote your kids' self-worth by giving them positive self-talk they will internalize and make their own.

33

Lending an Ear and a Prayer

In the early 1990s my wife had the stressful job of managing a small, family-owned Christian bookstore. It was her first management job, so she occasionally came home and vented her frustrations about the challenges she faced. At least once a week I listened to her tell me about some issue she was having with a vendor or employee. Fortunately, she had come to a wise and business-savvy individual, so I had an abundance of advice to offer. Why else would she be telling me all this if she didn't want to hear my opinions, right?

After hearing about five or ten minutes of her woes, I'd say something like, "Okay, this is really easy. Let me tell you what to do. First, you call the vendor and ask for the manager. Then you explain that your shipment was late and it cost you a valuable customer. Then..."

That's normally about as far as I got before she got frustrated. She told me that she didn't want a lecture, that she just wanted me to listen to her. I only had to go through this about 40 or 50 more times before the lesson finally sank in: My wife didn't want me to fix her problem. She just wanted me to listen without comment or judgment.

I wanted to come to the rescue and fix everything because that's what we men do. But my wife didn't want to be rescued. She wanted a friend she could share her burdens with. She wanted me to empathize with her.

Now, all these years later, my kids come to me with their problems too, and thanks to those conversations with my wife earlier in our marriage, I have a better idea of what to do.

First, I listen. I don't try to fix their problem. I just let them get it all out of their systems. With kids, sometimes that process can go on for about three or four hours if you let it, so I do set some limits on how long they can vent. But for a while at least, my job is sitting beside them and nodding.

Second, I empathize and let them know I have been in either the same situation or one that's very similar. My kids love hearing stories about their mother and me when we were young, so that's the time for me to pull out one of my old stories about a time when I blew it, lost the contest, embarrassed myself in front of a crowd, hurt myself, broke something, or whatever experience I had that was similar to theirs.

Only then might I offer a small bit of counsel. If they've erred in some way, I might challenge them to try to fix the problem. If they lost an opportunity, I might suggest they try again. If something is broken, we talk about how it might be replaced or repaired. Sometimes they're open to hearing some input, but sometimes the pain is still too close and I have to wait for a better opportunity.

But I don't always have the answer. Sometimes there is nothing I can say that will make it all better. Those are the times when I put my arms around them, hug them, and say, "Let's pray about it." They need to know that there is a bigger power than Dad. There is a God who cares and who is willing to take their concerns in his hands.

If you don't know the right words to say when praying with your kids, well, welcome to the club. There have been many times when I haven't known what to say either, so I usually led with that.

"Lord, I don't have a clue what to say or how to fix this…"

The really cool part about this process is seeing my kids internalize that faith. Now the prayer requests go both ways. When I had hernia surgery not long ago, I told my kids, "Guys, I'm really hurting right now. Would you do me a favor and pray for your dad?"

Since prayer has been part of our daily interaction for years, they don't have any problem with stepping up when somebody else has a need. And I don't know about you, but I'm the type of guy who needs a lot of prayer and wants to surround himself with praying people. If those people happen to be a part of my family, I can't help feeling pretty good about that.

The Takeaway

Promote your kids' faith by letting them see your relationship with God and your dependence on him.

34

The Date You Don't Want to Miss

My daughter and I began attending daddy/daughter dances about four or five years ago. Each dance we've gone to has had a different theme. Last year the theme was Western, so we were supposed to dress up like cowboys. I don't keep a lot of Western clothing on hand, but I do own a pair of cowboy boots that I bought on a whim back in the '90s because I somehow became convinced that I really, really, really needed them. I wore them once or twice, and they sat in my closet until the dance last year. So I added a plaid shirt and some jeans to the boots and came up with what I hoped passed for a cowboy outfit.

The previous year, the theme was the '50s. That look was a bit trickier for me to pull off since the greased-back pompadour is such an integral feature of the '50s, and I'm what some people might refer to as follicly challenged. If I wanted that '50s look, I knew I'd have to wear a wig, and that wasn't going to happen. I was going to have to create a '50s look that didn't involve hair. I decided to take my cue from Marty McFly in *Back to the Future* and donned some blue jeans and white tennis shoes.

This year the theme was the '80s, which was a lot closer to my own experience and comfort zone. To be honest, my outfit this year looked a lot like my '50s costume did a couple years ago—blue jeans, a button-down shirt, and white tennis shoes. I guess I'm really not that creative in coming up with theme-based costumes. In my defense, I did add a skinny tie to the ensemble to dress it up a bit.

That look was very comfortable for me because that's pretty much the style of clothing I was wearing until a couple of years ago, when someone informed me I was decades out of style. My thinking was that we got it right with the music and clothing styles back in the '80s, so why change?

When my date and I arrived at the gymnasium, I could tell the planners of the event went all out. The walls were decked out with huge images of Pac-Man. Rubik's Cubes and vinyl LPs served as centerpieces on the tables. And MC Hammer, Whitney Houston, and Michael Jackson played on the sound system. When I looked around at the dads and daughters attending, there were mullets and big hair as far as the eye could see. It was a little slice of heaven.

My daughter and I danced together, ate junk food, drank soda, danced some more, and then ate more junk food. It was glorious. I enjoyed spending time with my daughter, and she enjoyed having her dad all to herself.

The daddy/daughter dance is a fun night out, but I believe it's also important to a daughter's development. In a large part, a girl's relationship with her father will determine the type of relationship she will have with her husband someday. If she grows up interacting with a kind man who treats her respectfully, that's most likely the type of guy she's going to feel the most comfortable with in the future.

And just to let you in on a little daddy secret: I love the idea of making it hard on her future suitors by giving them a lofty ideal to live up to. When I'm out with my daughter, I open the door for her when she gets in and out of the car, and I treat her like a lady the whole night. If she's used to being treated like she's special, she's less likely to put up with rudeness and disrespect from young men who might be interested in her. Something within her will immediately recognize behavior that doesn't resonate with who she has been raised to believe she is. She will automatically think she deserves better, which is a great thing because I happen to be of the same opinion.

If I can help her have a better chance of finding happiness by demonstrating the way a date is supposed to behave, I will have accomplished something worthwhile with my life. If I can do that while doing the Electric Slide and eating Pac-Man cupcakes, then it's a win-win situation.

The Takeaway

Promote your daughter's relational success by demonstrating what a good man looks like so she will demand the same when she selects her spouse.

The Buck Stops Here

As I was waiting to board a plane in Denver, I struck up a conversation with a couple who were headed back home after vacationing with their kids. Their six-year-old boy and seven-year-old girl were happily bouncing all over the place, still excited from their four-day skiing trip. Dad had just come back to the gate area loaded up with toys and trinkets from the airport gift shop.

When he handed the gifts to the children, I could tell it gave him pleasure to see his kids happy. I commented that it is easy to spend money on your kids, and both of the parents readily agreed.

"Well, it's not such a bad thing to loosen up a little bit and buy a few souvenirs for them while you're on vacation," I said.

"This is how he is all the time," the wife commented, smiling at her husband.

The husband grinned and said, "Guilty as charged!"

"He just can't say no to them," she bragged. "Whatever they want, they get!"

The husband nodded in agreement. "I can't help it," he said. "They're my kids and I love 'em!"

Listening to all of this, I was thinking, *Oh, no! If you love your kids, you might want to rethink this. Giving them everything they want is one of the worst things that can happen to their character.*

Unchecked abundance doesn't create good character. If anything, it produces a sense of entitlement that shackles your children in every area. If they grow up *getting* everything, they will forevermore *expect* everything.

The recession of 2008–2011 should have taught us that hard times are inevitable. When overindulged kids finally have to experience tough times—and they will—they won't be able to cope. They will always expect someone else to provide for them and bail them out. They will be programmed to believe that one's sustenance magically shows up whenever they need it or want it, and when it doesn't, they will feel discontent and resentful. Their future spouses will have to deal with their out-of-control spending habits or their constant demands, which will lead to unending marital friction.

What part of that scenario would any parent want for their kids? But that's exactly what parents who overindulge their children are guaranteeing for them.

Some parents rationalize their behavior, saying they have the extra money to spend. But being able to afford the extra expenditures isn't the issue. The main concern is teaching your children to respect the value of money so they can have a better shot at success in life.

Having a surplus of money doesn't mean you need to throw off restraint—rather, just the opposite. It means you need to demonstrate more self-control. Even though the multimillionaire John D. Rockefeller had more cash than we can imagine, he raised his children to value money. Instead of giving each of them a fat allowance, he paid them for specific household chores, such as killing flies, sharpening pencils, or doing small repairs. In addition, they had to keep precise ledgers of their income and expenditures.

And it's not just the wealthy who overindulge their kids. I see mid- to lower-income families do it every day by redefining luxuries as necessities. The kids must have the latest video game, TV, cell phone, or computer. They must go on vacation. They must wear designer label clothes. There is no end to the materialism, and instead of defining the financial boundaries, many parents enable the greed.

So how much stuff is okay to give your kids? That depends on the child and the family, but asking the question is a great start. It's the parents who never think about the subject that worry me. When it comes to teaching your kids about money, as the old saying goes, more is caught than taught. Your kids are observing your behavior and learning from your actions.

What have you either intentionally or unintentionally taught your children about money today? This week? This month? It pays to invest in your kids' success by modeling a lifestyle of frugality and financial responsibility. And when you see them imitating the prudent behavior you have demonstrated, well, you just can't buy that kind of satisfaction.

The Takeaway

Promote financial responsibility in your children by modeling frugality, showing financial restraint, and recognizing the value of money.

Part 6

PREVENT

May these words of my mouth
and this meditation of my heart
be pleasing in your sight,
Lord, my Rock and my Redeemer.

PSALM 19:14

36

Disconnection Through Inaction

My brother, Fred, was about ten years older than me, and I had always looked up to him when we were growing up. He was a gifted athlete, and I admired not only his basketball skills but also the attention those skills brought. His name and picture regularly appeared in the local paper, which always seemed to praise his athletic prowess and domination of the basketball court.

Fred spent time teaching me how to dribble and shoot a basketball, throw a football, and catch a baseball in my glove. There was nothing related to sports that he didn't know how to do.

Then Fred moved away to go to college, met a girl, and started a family of his own. He had two awesome boys, and he made it a point to be involved in every aspect of their lives. He passed on his knowledge and passion for sports to them, sometimes even coaching their Little League teams and making it to most of their games. He bragged loudest and longest about their achievements, whether that meant artwork, grades, or sports.

Unfortunately, Fred made some bad life-choices that resulted in his moving away from his family and living on his own in a small, two-bedroom apartment. The time he spent with his boys was reduced dramatically. Part of the problem might have been that he worked the night shift in a meat processing plant. When he got home in the morning, he was dead-tired, so he watched a little TV and then went to bed and slept most of the day. At first he made sure he saw his boys on their birthdays and holidays, but as the years passed, even those days seemed to slip by without him making a visit.

I was busy with my own life, so I rarely spoke to Fred, and since he lived several states away, I hadn't seen him in a very long time. In these days of instant access using Facebook, Twitter, Instagram, email, texting, and so forth, it's hard to remember just how out of touch people used to get before we had all that stuff. You could grow up with someone and talk to them every day, but then when one of you moved, you might not ever see each other again. At best, you might visit occasionally, but usually the relationship settled down to talking on the phone or exchanging letters every now and then.

When my speaking career began taking off in the late '90s, I started traveling all over the country, and I viewed that travel as an opportunity to visit old friends and relatives when I was in their area.

When I was booked to do an event in the area where Fred lived, I made it a point to see him. It was wonderful seeing my big brother again. Fred and I had a lot of catching up to do, and we talked nonstop for hours.

By that time Fred's kids were almost grown. One was just starting college, and the other was about to graduate and start his career. I had known my nephews back when they were little boys, but I had no idea what kind of people they had grown up to be.

"What are your kids like?" I asked Fred.

Fred thought for a moment and replied, "One time when he was about four, I was putting my oldest to bed and he said, 'You dream of me, Daddy, and I'll dream of you,'" Fred said, beaming at the memory. It was easy to see that this was a special memory for him.

I smiled and commented that that was a wonderful memory. "But what are they like now?" I asked. "What kind of young men are they?"

Fred thought for a minute and then responded with another memory. "Once, when they were little..."

And that was all I was able to get out of him. The truth is, he had no idea how to answer that question because he hadn't taken the time to find out. He had allowed his relationship with his kids to gradually grow weaker until he hadn't the slightest idea how to describe them.

Sometimes relationships fail all at once. Most of the time, though, they tear apart a little bit at a time, especially if we aren't careful to tend them. I hope to leave behind a legacy of engagement and interaction with my kids. Not just when they're young, but as long as I'm alive. And when I'm gone, maybe they'll be able to say they knew me as well.

The Takeaway

Prevent disconnection with your children by making sure you regularly spend time with them. Don't allow external circumstances to dictate your degree of involvement.

37

More SkyMiles, Less Family

It's hard for me not to laugh whenever one of my clients wants to know if I'll make it to their event to speak. I've spoken at events with kidney stones lodged in my urinary tract. I've spoken at events when I've had severe food poisoning. I've done dozens of events with two broken ribs. I'm a show-must-go-on kind of guy. Come what may, you can bet I'm going to do everything in my power to be there for your event, even if that means I have to suffer a bit to do it.

Having said that, there have been some times when I haven't been able to make it. When we were expecting our daughter, I booked a Valentine's Day banquet at a church on February 13, her exact due date. In the interest of full disclosure, I told the pastor of the church that we were expecting our daughter that day, but I added that something like only 2 percent of all children are born on their due date, so barring her coming on that exact date, I'd definitely be there.

So naturally, my daughter came on her due date. I called the pastor from my wife's hospital room, apologized, and told him I wouldn't be able to make it after all. He congratulated me, told me it posed no problem, and promised he would book me again in the future.

I tried calling the pastor to apologize about a month later, but he never took my phone calls again. I hated letting him down, but when I measure being present for my child's birth against performing at a church Valentine's Day party, well, I kind of have to go with my child's birth.

Since then, I've traveled about a bazillion miles speaking all over the country. Countless times as I'm boarding flights, I see the guys with the Diamond Medallion tag on their luggage, and I never know whether to feel envious of them or sorry for them. On the one hand, they're the first ones to get upgraded to first class, but on the other hand, they have to travel 125,000 miles a year or more to earn that status. That's a lot of time spent away from home. When I talk to those Diamond Medallion folks, the story is often the same. Third or fourth marriage. Kids grown. Rarely see them or the grandkids. Not happy about it, but what's a guy to do?

Hearing things like that makes a guy think. I don't want to be an asterisk in my kids' lives. I don't want to be just some guy who sporadically appears and then disappears again.

The problem is that it's easy to say we need to put family first, but in practicality, it's hard to know where to draw the line between providing for your family and participating in it. Every working parent has to figure out how to define the line between the two.

I was speaking to Gary after I did an event at his association in Ohio a few years back. Gary told me that until ten years ago, he had been working as a construction supervisor, remodeling fast-food restaurants. The money was great, but he was on the road well over 300 nights a year, traveling from state to state on one job site after another. His wife put up with his schedule for years and then decided she'd had enough. She gave him the ultimatum that it was either the job or the family. He reasoned that he could always get another job, but his family was irreplaceable, so he gave his notice to his employer the next day.

I have turned down lots of dollars so I could celebrate holidays and my kids' birthdays. I look at it this way: How much money would I take to miss being in my kids' lives? What is the number? Because that's the deal we're making. We don't get another chance to do it right. Once the bus has left the station, it's gone.

I believe that when children grow up without a dad, it creates a hole in their hearts that they can spend the rest of their lives trying to fill. It's my job to prevent that damage from happening by showing up, by being physically, emotionally, and spiritually there for them.

That seems like a much better deal to me. And if I don't get upgraded to first class as much? You know, I think I can live with that.

The Takeaway

Don't let yourself become irrelevant and unimportant to your children. Instead, maintain a consistent and regular presence in their lives.

38

When to Win and When to Lose

It's not hard for most dads to understand the concept of letting kids fail for their own good. We know that we don't need to run to them to dry their tears every time they get knocked down on the field. We know that our kids need to fall down a few times so they'll learn not to trip. But some dads take it a bit further.

Stephen always had to best his daughter, Carol, in every sport, every board game, and every contest. She vividly remembers playing many basketball games with him when she was only nine or ten years old. He crushed her time and time again and then danced around the driveway, yelling and pumping his hands in the air in triumph after he won. This happened with whatever game they played together, no matter what age she was. That he was competing with someone just a fraction of his size and intelligence didn't matter to him. Stephen came to play, and he played to win.

One day she worked up the nerve to tell him how this made her feel and asked him why he had to always be the big winner.

"I'm toughening you up!" he said. "It's a cruel world out there and people are going to be mean, so you need to learn how to suck it up and take it!"

Unfortunately, Carol learned a different lesson. Instead of learning that the world is a hard, cruel place, she learned her father was a hard, cruel man. Instead of becoming tougher, she became wounded, and those wounds adversely affected her relationships with men thereafter. When she grew up and married, every other word her husband spoke was heard through the filter of her father's harsh voice. It took her years to overcome the negativity those experiences planted in her soul.

It's a wonderful thing to play with your kids, but when you become a dad, it's time to redefine "winning." Instead of shooting for the highest score, your new goal should be to get your child to improve her skill level and stretch her abilities. Your objective is to try to match your play with her level so she has a chance of competing with you. That means playing a little less competitively at first and letting her have the win sometimes.

So am I saying it is a good idea to throw games and let your kids win? Yes, but only some of the time. Letting your kids win all the time turns them into overindulged, spoiled little people who shouldn't be turned loose on society.

I believe there is a balance in winning and losing that trains kids to compete instead of trouncing them into bitterness and subjection. That can be accomplished by adjusting some of your interaction with them and letting them have a few victories as you play together.

How much should you let them win? What is the right win/loss ratio with your child? I'd have to say it depends on the child's age and ability. When they're young and just learning a game, I think letting them win 40 to 60 percent of the time is about right. At that percentage, they win enough to keep them interested in the game, and their skill level continues to grow. Losing 40 to 60 percent of the time keeps their pride in check while they strive to get better.

As they grow older and their skill increases, then by all means, go for it and make them earn their win! And how do you know when the time comes not to throw any games at all? You'll know as soon as their abilities begin to match your own. The game gets tougher for you, and you start sweating more. Then it's time to let go and show them what the old man can do.

And by the way, when I say let your kids win a bit, I'm not asking you to lie to your kids, but you don't need to tell them you're going easy on them either. I'm just asking you to not crush their spirits, and while you're at it, why not teach them something about how to take a loss? When they win, congratulate them and show them what it looks like to be a gracious loser. When they lose, ask them to return the same courtesy to you.

Remember that their skills and abilities are a reflection of all that you've taught them. All their achievements, accomplishments, and victories are yours as well. When they win, you win.

The Takeaway

Prevent the seeds of resentment and dysfunction in your children by redefining the term "winning" when competing with them. See yourself as your children's coach and not their competitor.

39

Stepping Up Instead of Stepping Out

Addison and Greg have a standing date every Friday and Saturday night. On Friday night they drop their baby off at Addison's dad's house and then go out drinking at their favorite watering hole. They keep the party going through Saturday night while the baby is cared for by his grandfather. On Sunday evening Addison and Greg come back to her dad's house to pick up their child. Addison's dad isn't happy about the situation, but what can he do? His daughter and her boyfriend like to party, and at least they have the sense to leave the baby with a trusted family member. Addison reasons that she and her boyfriend are young and have the right to enjoy life while they can. She has no plans to change her routine in the near future.

Their story reminds me of another young lady named Jessica who also liked the party life and had what some refer to as "commitment issues." By her early twenties, she had produced four children with four different men. None of the dads stuck around, so the grandparents were tasked with babysitting while their mom went out every other night. Jessica was fine with her life choices and saw no reason to change. When she lost her life in a drunk-driving accident, the children were left with no mother and their fathers scattered to the four winds. Once again, the grandparents had to step up and take responsibility for their daughter's foolishness.

The thing is, stories like these aren't that rare anymore. Almost anyone you meet can tell you about similar situations—young people who are biologically and legally adults start having children whom they refuse to raise themselves.

Thank God that sometimes there are grandparents who are willing to fill the void and care for these poor kids. Often, though, there are no relatives, and the state winds up taking charge of the children, placing them in foster care. Thank God there are foster parents who are willing to step up.

Stories like these make me wonder how anyone could have a child and not realize it is their responsibility to take care of him or her. When you become a parent, you are signing an invisible contract that says you are committing your life to the safety and well-being of your child. You are dedicating your existence to providing for the financial, physical, emotional, and spiritual needs of that little person.

It doesn't matter if you feel like going out. If doesn't matter if you've behaved yourself all week long and feel like you want to cut loose.

Sure, all dads and moms need a break, but going out and getting intoxicated—whether falling down drunk or lightly buzzed—is not the break that responsible parents take. Kids need someone to be the hero in their lives.

Sometimes that hero doesn't start off in the most ideal circumstances. Sometimes he has made some choices he isn't proud of. But a hero always comes around before it's too late. He makes the effort to right the wrongs he's committed. He steps up for the weak and helpless.

In parenting that means not only showing up for your kids but also staying put for them. It means reevaluating friendships that don't support your family. It means saying good-bye to habits and people that would entice you away from your family.

I don't like getting preachy, but honest to goodness, sometimes it needs to be said. Children don't need checked-out, inebriated, partying parents. Don't kid yourself into believing that there is any middle ground on this subject. The partying life is a slippery slope that sometimes ends in the grave. If you think that's extreme, I might argue that Jessica thought so too. And now her kids will grow up not remembering anything about her.

The Takeaway

Prevent and break the chain of generational substance dependency. A partying lifestyle is not compatible with parenting.

The Celebrity Dad

In mid-November 2002, Michael Jackson stood at the window of his room at Hotel Adlon in Berlin, waving to his adoring fans. A small crowd of admirers several stories below screamed and applauded the pop star as he smiled and gestured to them. At one point, Michael showed off his infant son to the crowd by dangling him over the window railing. Following the event, he was criticized widely for his carelessness regarding the safety of his child. He soon issued an apology for his actions, saying that he "got caught up in the excitement of the moment."

Maybe it's just me, but I can't imagine any level of excitement that would cause me to hang one of my kids out a window several stories high. In fact, I contend that any parent on this planet would know better than to do something like that. Well, any parent besides a celebrity, that is.

Celebrities sometimes seem to operate in a different reality from the rest of us, don't they? I recently read an article naming several movie stars who avoid bathing and using deodorant because they claim those activities are unhealthy. My question is, how about smelling someone else's BO all day? Is that healthy for the rest of us? Just wondering.

And when it comes to parenting, a lot of celebrities don't exhibit any more sense. I watched a news magazine interview as a rock-star parent espoused his views on proper parenting. "I want to make sure that my daughter gets her freak on. We [referring to his baby's mama] grew up in real repressive homes and we don't want that for our kids. Whatever they want to do, we're going to encourage them to do it!"

What a marvelous idea. Just let your kids do whatever they want.

In my view, that parenting philosophy will work out just fine, as long as you…

1. hand the kids over to nannies so you don't have to deal with the consequences of that decision, and
2. don't care about where your kids wind up in life.

It's what I call the Celebrity Parenting Method—the world's best-known, comprehensive method of destroying a child's life. Just leave them to their own devices, give them no training, surrender them to their own appetites and desires, and then watch them self-destruct. They will be holy terrors to all who know them when they're little, and when they reach their teenage years, they'll be out of control, self-destructive, noncontributing narcissists at best. At worst they'll be dead.

Fortunately, most of us can't off-load our kids to nannies. Most of us noncelebrity parents realize that the responsibility of training our kids lies with us—that if our children are going to grow up and become healthy, contributing members of society, we're going to need to invest in them.

Don't get me wrong. There are plenty of things we can learn from celebrities, such as skin care, hairstyles, singing, acting, and, um, skin care. But in regard to parenting, I've found it's wise to look in other places.

Attending the same church for years allowed my wife and me to observe several families that managed to produce awesome, well-adjusted young people with whom I would be proud to associate. Isn't that something? We're often told that families are going to be dysfunctional and kids are going to go astray no matter what we do.

But after watching these families for years, I've learned it is possible to create successful families with well-balanced kids. I've found that when you make a point of being relevant in your kids' lives while providing direction and structure, most of the time you wind up with people you actually like being around.

Unless, of course, your kids follow the Celebrity Personal Hygiene Method. But that will have to be another chapter in another book.

The Takeaway

Prevent your child's destruction by not leaving them to their own devices. Children need instruction and guidance if they are going to develop into responsible, giving adults.

41

The Wonder (Woman) of Halloween

Halloween has always been a fun time in my family. Some folks don't like it because it has pagan origins, but in our house, it's just "dress up and get candy" day.

When I was growing up, though, Halloween was a pretty scary time for me. Not because of all the ghosts and goblins and such, but because my mom made all my costumes. Every kid knows that a good Halloween costume has to be either scary or cool, and Mom's costumes fell short on both counts. I was that kid walking around the neighborhood wearing the nasty old worn-out sheet. It's hard to look like a ghost if your sheet is threadbare and has three years of slobber stains on it.

After a while, Mom just quit trying. She would send me out the door on Halloween night in my normal clothes and say, "Tell the neighbors you're dressed up like a kid who can't afford a costume."

The old hand-me-down costumes I got were worse than the ones Mom made. They wouldn't have been so bad if they all hadn't belonged to my sisters beforehand. It was humiliating wearing them around the neighborhood, and there was no talking my way out of it either. I tried convincing my friends that I was wearing Superman's summer outfit, but they knew a Wonder Woman costume when they were looking at it. So, thus outfitted, I would forage for goodies in my neighborhood. When I got home, I dumped out my trick-or-treat bag to see what I got, which was mostly candy. But every now and then, somebody would slip in an apple or popcorn ball. What's up with that?

All I wanted was chocolate. I was willing to wade through a few Smarties and SweeTarts, but making me trudge around the neighborhood dressed up like Wonder Woman for an apple just seemed wrong.

How tough is it to stock up on a few bags of Snickers or Twix anyway, for crying out loud?

The candy my parents were offering wasn't much better. The kids visiting my house got a handful of that peanut butter taffy wrapped in the black and orange wrappers. This was (and I believe still is) the nastiest and cheapest candy known to mankind. Back then, you could go out and buy a whole dump truck load of the stuff for about a buck seventy-nine, and it's even cheaper today.

The most miserable Halloween I've ever experienced, though, was after I was grown and had kids of my own. In 2004, I took my daughter trick-or-treating for the first time and enjoyed every minute of it. The following year, I was offered the opportunity to speak on Halloween night and had to decide how to invest my time. Did I need to go trick-or-treating again with my daughter or sacrifice that experience to provide for my family? It was a tough decision, but I went with putting food on the table. She was only three years old and wouldn't even miss me being there. That's what I told myself, anyway.

So I committed to do a comedy show at a church in Florida. Now, I understand that anytime you get paid to go somewhere and kid around with a bunch of folks, it's a good thing, and you ought to be thankful for the opportunity. But that night my heart felt heavy. It seemed everywhere I looked I saw dads with their kids. I missed being with my girl and having the chance to connect with her, and I regretted my decision to do the event. So I made a decision right then and there.

Never again would I miss a Halloween with my kids. Nor would I miss Easter or birthdays or recitals or any other special occasion. If I made a little less money as a result, then so be it.

My motivation for making that decision was only partially for my children's sake. The main reason was that I don't want to miss my children growing up. All the audiences, all the applause, and all the accolades in the world can't replace the joy of seeing the excitement on my kids' faces, hearing their laughter, and feeling the warmth of their company.

So next Halloween, look for me at your door with my kids, holding a bag and saying, "Trick or treat!" But don't expect me to be wearing the Wonder Woman costume. Not that I don't still have the legs for it.

The Takeaway

Don't let there be a hole in your calendar where memories and connection with your children should be. You deserve the pleasure of celebrating special times with your family.

42

Busy Being Busy

Think about how much of your life you spend choosing from the menu. We choose freely, but only from the selections that are right in front of us. One man goes to college, gets a degree, and enters a profession. Another man learns a trade and begins his own business. Another does neither and goes to work in the family business. I often see men in these roles and wonder what would have happened to them if they had switched places at birth. Would they still have taken the paths they did?

I think not. I think they most likely would have traded career paths when they traded families. They would have made different choices because the menu in front of them looked different and they would have selected one of the options given to them.

How much do we do every day simply because it is the norm in our circles? Take the way we raise our kids, for example. See if this sounds familiar:

Karen Johnson picks up her twelve-year-old daughter after school on Monday and takes her directly to cheerleading practice. She then drives to another school and picks up her eight-year-old son and drops him off at basketball practice. Her four-year-old daughter has been with her in the car all the while, so now Mom drives her to ballet practice, where they stay for the next hour. Then they get back in the car and pick up the other kids before rushing home for a quick bite. Then it's time to head back out again because the oldest daughter has modern dance lessons.

Tuesday looks a lot like Monday except the oldest daughter is dropped off for piano lessons after school and then goes to ballet and tap dance classes afterward. The youngest tags along again and gets dropped off for her gymnastics class. Dad drops off the son for his guitar lesson and then heads to the church, where he has a building committee meeting.

On Wednesday, the boy has tennis lessons and the oldest girl has lacrosse practice. The whole family meets afterward for a hurried dinner, and then it's off to church they go. On Thursday, it's more lessons, classes, and practice. Can you guess what their Friday looks like?

Throughout the year, the sports and types of classes change, but the pace remains the same. Countless families across the nation maintain this lifestyle year in and year out. But I wonder if anyone ever stops to ask, why are we doing this?

No doubt, we do it because we think it's the right thing to do. We believe we are giving our children more opportunity. But opportunity for what? Does it help them in college? Maybe. For a few very gifted students, there might be some scholarships available, but those cases are the exceptions, not the rule. The great majority of students won't qualify for a scholarship in sports, dance, or music. For all of us to commit this much energy and activity in the hope of getting a limited number of scholarships is akin to purchasing a very expensive lottery ticket.

So maybe it's for just the experience itself. But if that's the answer, then my question would be, what experience are we giving them? And does involvement in five or six activities a week mean your child is experiencing a better childhood? Better than being at home with your family?

It seems we're just ordering off the menu, that we're living lives of hectic activity because that is the standard these days. It's what everyone does with their kids, so we feel we're depriving our kids if they're not involved in as many activities as the family across the street.

But activity does not equal accomplishment. You can get to the end of your day (or life for that matter) having checked everything off your to-do list but missed everything important.

Please don't misunderstand me. I'm not asking you to cancel all your kids' activities. I'm merely recommending that you scale them back a bit. I'm suggesting the radical notion that time with you is just as important as playing team sports or taking ballet lessons. I'm saying that the lessons they will absorb by being with you will be just as valuable and worthwhile as whatever they can gain from learning a second instrument.

Don't feel bad setting limits on your kids' activities. Everyone needs boundaries. Your kids don't need the faucet turned wide open on activities any more than they need to be indulged in food, money, or entertainment.

Maybe it's time to order something that isn't on the menu. Maybe it's time to evaluate your family's priorities and needs and design a menu that best fits those. I can't promise you that you'll always like everything on the menu, but I can promise you that you won't be eating what someone else chose for you.

The Takeaway

Don't confuse the pursuit of completing your to-do list with having a successful family. Learn to set limits on extracurricular activities in favor of a more peaceful life for both you and your children.

Part 7

PERSIST

Let us not become weary in doing good, for at the proper time we will reap a harvest if we do not give up.

GALATIANS 6:9

43

Voted Most Likely to Be Unpopular

I found out early that I wasn't one of the popular kids in school. I wasn't even within shouting distance. To be popular, you had to have money or connections or good looks, and I had none of those things. I was zero for three. My mom shopped for my clothes at Kmart, my parents weren't exactly well connected, and my looks, well, let's just say the girls weren't exactly throwing themselves at me, and for good reason.

Back in those days, it was common for your mom to cut your hair, and I was no exception. Recently, I looked at my hair in some of my old school pictures, and for the first time in my life, I thought, *Wow, maybe Mom didn't know what the heck she was doing.*

And when I say I wore Kmart clothes, I don't mean top of the line, first-rate Kmart clothes. (Yes, there's a difference between the two types, and you wouldn't even ask if you ever had to wear them.) What I mean is, blue-light special, nobody-else-would-buy-them-so-we're-practically-giving-them-away Kmart clothes. So I wasn't ever voted Best-Dressed Kid or Most Likely to Become a Runway Model. Big surprise, huh?

The one thing I did have going for me was my burgeoning comedic talent. Slowly, I began to learn how to use my humor in social situations. When some kid took a shot at me on the playground, I found out a good one-liner could make him back off. Or even better, it could make him a friend. I learned that I had a bit of wit, and the other kids seemed to like it when I tossed out a joke in class. And I liked it because it got me the attention I craved.

Can I let you in on a little secret? All comedians begin telling jokes, wisecracking, and being funny so that they will be liked. All of them. Without exception. Hopefully a comedian will eventually gain some security and be able to use his comedic ability without needing to be validated all the time, but that's where it starts—with the desire to be liked.

But I found that I would have to say good-bye to that desire if I was going to be a good dad, because being a good leader isn't about being popular. It's about making tough decisions and being man enough to take the heat from an unpopular call.

"No, you can't go to that party."

"No, we aren't going on vacation this year."

"No, you aren't going to that movie."

"No, you're not getting that video game."

"No, you aren't taking that job."

"No, you don't get to lay around the house all summer and do nothing."

You have to be able to make decisions for the betterment of the individual and family and not worry about how well those decisions will go over with the masses. Think of being a dad as the polar opposite of being a politician.

If your principal motivation is to be liked, to be the popular parent, to make everyone around you happy, then you're in for a tough time, and your kids are going to be the ones who suffer for it. Sure, everyone will be happy at first, but that won't last long for two simple reasons.

1. The demands don't stop. When everyone around you senses that you're an easy mark, they'll just keep on coming.
2. Every action produces a consequence. Kids who don't learn to respect boundaries grow into adults who are out of control and a menace to themselves and everyone around them.

Good dads know it's more important to be their kids' dad than to be their friend. Good dads don't need to win popularity contests. They have their eyes on the long-term benefits rather than short-term ego gratification.

The bottom line is, your kids don't need you to be their friend. They will have lots of friends throughout their lives. Hopefully, if all goes according to plan, they'll only have one dad. Make sure you're the type of dad who stays true to the course, sticks to the plan, and is the leader his family needs.

The Takeaway

Setting a behavioral standard for your children and continuing to uphold it are among the most essential parts of leadership and fatherhood.

44

Putting the Kids to Bed...Eventually

One of the benefits of my kids being a little bit older now is that it's a lot easier to put them to bed. When they were little, their bedtime was eight p.m. sharp—no exceptions, no excuses, end of story. Which meant if my wife and I stayed focused and started early, we usually had them in bed around eleven or twelve. No later than one or two. Definitely before sunrise.

The process of getting our kids to bed was long and complicated. Entire civilizations rose and fell in the time it took to just get them into their pajamas.

The first step was to brush their teeth. This process took about 20 minutes because after seven p.m., my kids lost all resemblance to rational human beings and started running around like escaped monkeys.

Picture this. There I am with one of my arms around the waist of my four-year-old son, who is gleefully trying to tear the shower curtain down. With my other hand I'm holding a toothbrush with just a fraction of the toothpaste I originally put on it. The rest of the toothpaste is now decorating the bathroom wall, tub, and counter. While my son happily flops around in my arms like a fish in the bottom of a bucket, I'm randomly poking a toothbrush in the general direction of his mouth, hoping to somehow hit it when it's open. After a while, when I feel satisfied that I've given it my best shot, I pronounce his teeth officially brushed, and we move on to donning the jammies.

Dressing squirmy, wiggling little bodies in pajamas consists of grabbing a flailing arm or leg and thrusting it into whatever part of the pajamas I'm holding at the time. The rule is, the kids have to wear pajamas to bed. It doesn't matter if they are wearing them correctly or not.

After we manhandle the kids into their jammies, it's time for the bedtime story. The reading of the story would only take about five minutes if everyone would keep their mouths shut and just listen to the story. But for every page read, there are about 50 relevant, urgent questions that must be asked and answered before the story can continue.

"Daddy, is Curious George a bad guy?"

"What is his friend's name?"

"Are the police going to put him in jail?"

"Is Curious George friends with Dora the Explorer?"

Sometimes I would just ignore the questions and keep reading. Sometimes I would ignore the questions and imagine I was on a tropical island far, far away. Sometimes I would hide in my closet until my wife got the kids in bed.

But I digress.

Finally, when the story is read, it's prayer time. This process involves a lengthy period of time when the kids roll all over the floor, intermittently mumbling scraps of prayer with their sentences punctuated by random incidents and observations.

"Dear Lord, thank you for Mommy and Daddy." Roll, roll, roll, giggle, grab the dog, giggle. "And, dear Lord, thank you for Scrappy." Roll, roll, roll, leg flops onto other child, fight breaks out, dispute resolved, prayer starts over from the beginning. "Dear Lord, thank you for Mommy and Daddy..."

At long last, the prayers are finished, and it's finally time for little people to actually be in their beds. Hooray! Huzzah! Hallelujah! But no, it only looks like the job is complete. We're still far from the finish line. It's a lot like a cease-fire in the Middle East. It's best not to get your hopes up.

At the very instant the lights go off, and not a moment before, gastrological processes start taking place in tiny tummies that necessitate urgent trips to the bathroom. By this time, we parents are already downstairs, so there is no adult supervision in the bathroom. Consequently, entire Broadway shows are performed in front of the bathroom mirror. Complicated scientific experiments are conducted using running water from the faucet. Creative works of art are produced with vast amounts of toilet paper.

This is about the time I turn into a raging maniac and the kids sense that if they want to see another sunrise, the hour has truly come for them to get into bed. Afterward, my wife and I have about 20 minutes of peace before we go to bed and then get up the next day and do the whole thing over again.

It's a classic Shakespearean struggle. It's an epic contest of good versus evil. It's a clash of wills on a galactic scale. It's everyday parenting.

That was then. Now we are past those days, and bedtime is a lot easier. And I'm just kidding about hiding in the closet while my wife did all the work. The truth is, I stayed the course every night because I knew it was important. I believe that dads need to be part of the process and—this is the important part—keep being a part. It's too easy for dads to chip in once in a while and then slack off. Kids need to see that Dad is part of the day-to-day parenting process. He is not an addendum. He's not an afterthought. He is not a parental accessory. He is structurally essential. He is indispensable.

Remember, Dad, it's not the gigantic, one-time effort that creates success in any area in life, but the consistent, daily effort, day in and day out.

The Takeaway

Do not grow weary and lax in maintaining a daily, structured schedule for your kids.

Running the Good Race

By now, you've probably heard about Team Hoyt, the amazing father-and-son team consisting of Rick, who is a quadriplegic with a severe form of cerebral palsy, and his father, Dick, who pushes, pulls, and pedals him through endless miles of grueling races. You may have seen pictures of Rick being pushed in a specially designed wheelchair with his eyes closed and head tilted back, and his father just behind him, doggedly pushing him onward. You probably know they have participated in more than a thousand races over a 31-year span. You might know that after running in a few marathons, they graduated to full triathlons—events so challenging and daunting that few able-bodied people ever dare to enter them.

You've probably heard that they ran their last marathon in Boston in 2014 and that they were greeted by hordes of people who cheered them as they crossed the finish line. You may have seen pictures of the life-size bronze statue of them that sits just a few yards from the starting line of the Boston Marathon, commemorating their enormous athletic achievements and their contribution to disability awareness.

Maybe you heard that many years before then, Dick and Judy Hoyt took their baby, Rick, to be examined by specialists, and they were advised to place him in an institution because there was no hope of him recovering or living a "normal life." But the young couple realized that even though Rick couldn't speak, he was still very intelligent, and they undertook the task of teaching him the alphabet at home. They had a special computer built that was designed so that Rick could type words by using his head to activate a control mounted in the headrest of his chair. It was with great anticipation that his parents waited to see what his first words would be. Would he write "I love you, Mom and Dad"? Would it be "It's great to finally be able to talk"? His first two-word sentence proved not only that he had wit and intelligence but also that he was an avid sports fan. It happened the Boston Bruins were in the Stanley Cup that year, so Rick's first words were "Go Bruins!"

Maybe you've heard all those stories by now, but I wonder if anybody ever thinks about the miles—the grueling, thankless, painful miles that were run long before any of the recognition, support, and fame arrived. I wonder if anyone imagines all the times Rick fell out of his chair and all of the times Dick gently scooped him up and placed him back in. I wonder if anyone thinks about what was going through Dick's mind as he placed one foot in front of the other, carrying not only his own weight, but that of his son as well.

Mile after unglamorous mile. Endless stretches of lonely, arduous road with no one cheering, no one encouraging them. Only the road and the sounds of Dick's breath and his feet hitting the pavement. They were completely invisible to those of us waiting at the finish lines.

I think it's a good metaphor for fatherhood sometimes. A lot of dads are running a race with their kids metaphorically strapped to their backs. Sometimes the child has a health challenge. Sometimes the challenge is emotional. Sometimes it's relational, spiritual, or financial. And since we're still in the middle of the race, there is no one to cheer us on. We can't see the big finish. All we can see is the punishment of the road. And we keep on running. Because that's what a good dad does.

A few dads give up and walk off. The race was too tough, too grueling. They beg off, excuse themselves, and disappear.

But some persist. They want to get to the end of the race. They want to see their kids' expressions when they win—when they grow up, get married, have kids of their own, get jobs, start businesses, and start running their own races.

They do so because they know that kids need their dads to keep pushing them forward. Kids need their fathers to keep running the race with them. They need to be able to look over at any point in the race and see their dad running, sweating, and straining forward toward the finish line right along with them.

So the good dads persist because the race is worth enduring all the miles of hardship, and the victory is worth every bit of pain.

The Takeaway

Your kids are counting on you to keep pace with them as they face their daily challenges. Let them see your tenacity and courage as you run beside them.

46

The Day My World Shook

I woke from a sound sleep at about 5:35 a.m. in a dark hotel room in Muncie, Indiana, on April 18, 2008. A sensation I had never before experienced nudged me awake, and I lay in the bed for a moment or two, trying to figure out what was happening. My whole bed—no, make that the whole room—was shaking. At first I thought maybe a train was going past or maybe a large aircraft was flying low overhead, but neither of those theories seemed quite right. I got out of bed and looked out the window, but everything outside appeared normal. Then it dawned on me that I was experiencing my very first earthquake.

It's kind of funny to me that I wasn't all that frightened. Maybe I should have been, but it didn't seem all that bad. The earthquake wound up registering 5.4 on the Richter scale, which is enough for you to notice but doesn't usually cause much damage. The tremors continued for a good while, but eventually they subsided as suddenly as they had appeared. My main thought after it was over was that I had a great story to tell my wife later on. After the excitement wore off, I was able to go back to bed and get a couple more hours of sleep.

The first thing I did when I woke up again was reach for my phone, which had been turned off the whole night. Turning my phone off was unusual for me, and I have only done it maybe once or twice in my entire career.

I dialed my home phone number, and that was the moment my life changed. My daughter, Faith, who was six years old at the time, answered the phone and chatted to me for a little while, and then she handed the phone to my wife.

"Honey," she began, "I need to tell you something, and it's not going to be good. The reason I let you talk to Faith first was so that you could hear that she's all right."

I sensed something was wrong, and anxiety gripped my heart. "What is it?" I demanded. "What happened?"

My wife continued in a calm voice, "Last night Faith had a seizure and had to go to the hospital."

I was stunned and couldn't get the questions out fast enough. "A seizure? What do you mean? What happened? Was it bad?"

"Yes, honey, it was bad. She had a grand mal seizure and lost consciousness. I spent the whole night up at the hospital with her."

"Oh, no!" I said, choking back a sob. "My little girl!" I can't begin to tell you what it feels like to be almost 600 miles away when a catastrophe hits your family. I mentally berated myself for not having my phone on all night and for not being there when they needed me.

When I got back home, we visited a pediatric neurologist and were told that this might have been a one-time incident. We learned many children have one seizure but then are never troubled with another one for the rest of their lives. The doctor told us that if we made it for a year without her having another seizure, the odds were in our favor that she wouldn't have another one. So for a year we prayed and dared to hope.

Twelve months and one week later, she had her second grand mal. She was taken to the hospital again, and the MRI results weren't good. The doctor told us our daughter had epilepsy. We came to understand that "epilepsy" is a catchall term that means that someone has had two or more seizures and is likely to have more.

Most people don't know a lot about epilepsy, and there is a good reason for that. It is one of the most underfunded, least understood, and least recognized of all neurological disorders. Seizure disorders affect more people than Parkinson's, multiple sclerosis, cerebral palsy, and muscular dystrophy combined. One in 26 people will develop a seizure disorder sometime in their lifetime. Three million people in the US are affected, and it is estimated that an additional 300,000 cases will be diagnosed this year. It can strike anyone, anywhere, anytime. In 70 percent of the cases, there is no known cause.

Our family has spent the past seven years trying to live normal lives while battling this invisible enemy. About once a week a silent, vicious villain sneaks up and steals my bright, ebullient, loving, kindhearted daughter from us for two to five minutes. It's horrific.

Over the years we have patiently endured a plethora of well-meaning friends and family members who pepper us with a host of questions and suggested cures.

Do you think it had anything to do with her vaccinations? We don't know. Maybe. There's not a lot of research that supports that though. *Is it genetic?* No. Nobody in either of our families has ever had anything close to this. *Have you tried nutritional supplements or home remedies or alternative medicine?* Yes. At first we didn't because we thought an answer was right around the corner, but as the years rolled by, we became more open to alternative options. We've tried just about every homemade remedy you can imagine and several you can't.

We did all of that while exploring various pharmaceutical solutions. That process takes a long time because you have to increase the dosage slowly, give it some time to see if it is having any effect, and then reduce the dosage ever so slowly when it doesn't work.

And still my daughter has seizures.

If you are one of those parents who have never had anything bad happen to their children, then good for you. I hope you are always able to say that. But if you're not, if your situation is similar to ours, then you need to know that I wrote this part of the book for you.

This is the longest chapter in the book and the one I didn't want to write. This is the part of myself that I would like to keep hidden from everybody. But I'm telling this story for one reason, and that is to encourage you to persist. To keep on looking for answers for your child. To keep on fighting for your little one. Keep on no matter what. When you don't feel like it. When you've run out of faith. When there is no reason to hope. Continue to fight. Continue to hope. And most of all, continue to believe.

It's natural to wonder why God would allow something bad to happen to your child. You wouldn't be quite normal if you didn't question where God was in the midst of your child hurting.

But there is another perspective you might not have considered.

Maybe there was a child who needed a strong advocate, someone who refused to quit, someone who would persist as long as they had breath in their body.

Perhaps you are the answer. You. Even though you can't see the way. Even though you are insufficient. Even though you are out of strength. You have been placed in your child's life to help. You are God's merciful hand in your child's life. You are the miracle. Maybe you're not the miracle you want for your child. Maybe you're not what you think your child needs. But you're still the miracle God has provided—if you persist. If you don't give in to despair.

You are stronger than you know, and there is more strength yet for those who are willing to call out to God for help. Your world might shake and tremble. It might threaten to crash in around you, but you will continue to stand and fight for your child because that is who you are and who your child needs you to be.

The Takeaway

Never give up on finding solutions for your children's challenges. Continue to fight for them as long as there is a battle to be fought or a breath in your body.

47

How Kids Spell Love

It's important to know your strengths and weaknesses. One of my strengths is that I'm a natural performer. I love to be in front of crowds, and I've been able to make a good living by establishing myself as a keynote speaker who is fun and entertaining and who provides helpful tips for people in their business and personal lives.

My weakness is that I'm not a slow-burning lightbulb that lasts forever. I'm a flashbulb that burns brightly for a shorter amount of time. My programs are high-energy and fun, but they last for only a little while because it is difficult to sustain that level of energy forever. That's why I never do all-day events. The longest program I ever do lasts maybe three or four hours. Most of the time I speak for about an hour. I'm a keynote speaker, not a clinician.

That trait is pretty typical of my personality. I'm a sprinter, not a long-distance runner. I always start strong, but it's a challenge for me to maintain the same level of intensity and energy throughout a long project.

I've noticed that a lot of dads have the same tendency in their parenting. They start off active and engaged when the kids first arrive. They attend their recitals, coach them in sports, and go to their games. But then these dads get a little older, and life intervenes. The demands of work gradually increase, and they don't spend quite as much time with their kids.

Don't get me wrong. I understand there are times when the ox is in the ditch and a dad has to drop everything and turn his attention to getting his means of provision back on the road. But those times should be the exception, not the rule.

There might be a few days or even a season when both you and your family have to sacrifice time together to meet your financial obligations or needs, but those times can't become the norm. If they do, the whole point of working becomes obsolete. Your family adapts to not having you around and learns that your presence isn't necessary. Even worse, they come to believe that they are not your priority.

That's a horrible lesson for your kids, especially when the opposite is true—an engaged, loving father is essential to a child's development. You don't hear that perspective very often these days, but it's a fact.

I've been guilty of putting the cart before the ox plenty of times myself. It's easy to become lost in other pursuits and forget that your main job is showing up for your family. Somebody once said that the way kids spell love is T-I-M-E. It's not spelled M-O-N-E-Y. It's not spelled W-O-R-K. It's about a dad investing his time in his kids. If you claim that your family is your priority, then you have to show up. And even more important, you need to keep showing up.

If you want to make an impact on your kids, if you want to be relevant in their lives, if you want to leave a meaningful legacy, then you need to recognize that success in any endeavor isn't about one grandiose act. It's not a flashbulb. It's about being a steady, long-lasting lightbulb and contributing a consistent daily effort over the long haul. Being a successful dad means guarding your time with your kids and steadfastly seeking a healthy balance between work and family.

I love my job and am grateful that I get to speak and write for a living, but can I let you in on a little secret? I have learned that work will always be tapping on my shoulder, demanding my attention. It never gives up. Something always needs doing.

But my kids? Well, that's a different story. They will only be around for a little while, so to me, that means I need to make sure that work doesn't steal my time from them. It means I need to persist in being the type of dad who is present in their lives so they have no doubt about my priorities.

The Takeaway

Being a good father is not about the flashy, one-time play. It's about the long game.

48

A Hero's Secret Support

In *The Seven Powers of Success,* I tell the story of one of my heroes, the amazing Bill Porter. Bill was an unassuming, quiet man who gained worldwide recognition because of the inspirational way he lived his life. He wasn't a rock star, movie star, or athlete. Vocationally speaking, he was just a normal guy, but such was his tenacity, persistence, and courage that his story has been told numerous times in various media, including newspapers, television, and books. The Emmy award-winning actor and playwright William H. Macy heard about Bill and wrote a screenplay for *Door to Door,* a movie about Bill's life, which was released in 2002.

Bill was born on September 9, 1932, in San Francisco to Ernest and Irene Porter. As their son began to grow, Ernest and Irene began noticing some troubling developmental problems. They took their concerns to their family doctor, who recognized the symptoms and diagnosed Bill with cerebral palsy.

Cerebral palsy is a disorder that is believed to be caused by oxygen deprivation to the brain during birth or by damage to the parts of the brain that control movement in the fetal stage of development. Symptoms often include difficulty speaking, muscle weakness or stiffness, and poor coordination.

At the time when Bill was diagnosed, the affliction was still widely misunderstood and mistreated. Bill's parents visited a number of doctors and specialists and were told by most that Bill would most likely be mentally disabled and be institutionalized his whole life.

Ernest and Irene were devastated when they learned of Bill's condition. But they were unwilling to accept this pronouncement of doom by the experts, so they made it their life's mission to care for Bill and help him realize his potential. They believed that Bill was a gift from God and restructured their lives to educate themselves about cerebral palsy and help Bill overcome his disability.

During the height of the Great Depression, Bill's father made the bold decision to quit his job as an outside salesman so he could learn more about the special needs of his son. Both he and Irene took jobs at a school for special-needs children in San Francisco called the Berry School.

In the evenings, Ernest and Irene worked regularly with Bill, using exercises to improve his muscle coordination, and speech therapy to improve his ability to communicate. Under their tutelage, Bill's abilities improved and his confidence grew. They fostered a positive mental attitude in Bill that enabled him to excel as one of the top salesmen for Watkins Inc., a manufacturer of household goods that relies heavily on door-to-door sales.

When I look at Bill Porter, it's impossible for me not to be impressed with his tenacity, perseverance, courage, and strength. But I wonder how many people look behind Bill to see how he became who he was. I've never seen a hero who didn't have heroes standing behind him. I've never seen someone great who didn't have at least one person who believed in him somewhere in his past. There is no such thing as a Lone Ranger—somebody who stands alone in their achievement. Shoot, even the Lone Ranger had Tonto.

Without taking anything away from Bill, it's easy to see that a large part of the reason he was able to become so successful was that he had passionate, involved parents who actively invested and believed in him. They committed their entire lives to being the support system he needed so that when it was his time to fight his fight, he was already equipped with all the tools his challenge would require.

I've been talking about Bill's story to crowds for years, but the part that still gets to me is the way Bill's father set his own career and ego aside to work menial jobs at a special-needs school for the sole purpose of helping his son. That kind of dad doesn't make the headlines. That kind of dad is easy to overlook, and in most cases, the world never hears his name or knows about his sacrifice.

But that kind of recognition doesn't matter to that kind of dad. He knows that the recipients of his sacrifice will always know and remember what their success has cost him. And they will continue to bless his name and honor him because of it.

The Takeaway

Continue to be your child's advocate and champion. Your little heroes are counting on your support and encouragement.

Envisioning Your Destination

The first page in my notebook shows a bride holding a bouquet of pink and white roses. The next page is a picture of another bride in a long, flowing white dress as she is escorted down the aisle by her father. The page after that shows an older man and younger man wearing tuxedos, shaking hands on the younger man's wedding day. The following page has a picture of an older gentleman sitting on the ground, surrounded by his three grandchildren. The next page has a picture of an older couple walking hand in hand in the woods underneath a canopy of red, orange, and yellow leaves.

All these images represent pages in what I call my vision notebook. In *The Seven Powers of Success*, I make the argument that the Power of Vision is an indispensable part of anyone's success journey—whether financial, professional, physical, or familial. Vision is knowing where you want to wind up and why you want to get there. If you don't have a solid vision, you won't know where you want to go, and you won't recognize your target even if you happen to get close to it.

Having a solid vision enables you to manage your time and effort so you will arrive where you want when you want. A vision isn't a pipe dream or fantasy. It's not wanting to be rich and famous. It's not wanting to win the lottery. It is identifying specific, situational markers that you want to see happen for yourself, your family, or your organization.

Once you identify what you want and why you want it, creating a vision notebook is a great way to keep your vision in front of you. A vision notebook is a binder with pages of pictures that represent specific items that comprise your vision. It's a powerful tool because by looking at it regularly, you are reminding yourself of what kind of person you would like to be, where you want to see yourself, and why you are doing what you do.

I made mine by Googling pictures that represent things I want or events I want to see happen in my lifetime. I want to be there for both of my children's weddings. I want to live long enough to know my grandchildren and for them to know me. I want my marriage to last and flourish throughout our golden years. These pictures in my vision notebook remind me that I am running a marathon, that I have to live my life now in such a way that will increase my odds of seeing those events one day.

No, there are no guarantees. Anything could happen to prevent any one of these things from happening. But I know that *not* paying attention to my health will almost certainly decrease the odds of my living long enough to be a part of those events. I know that *not* respecting and nourishing my relationships with my family will lead to the decay of those relationships. It is up to me to do my part to keep all my relationships strong and to prevent strife and disagreements from separating me from any member of my family.

The biggest benefit of the vision notebook is that it keeps me on track and helps me to persist in doing the things that will bring me success in the areas that are important to me. It reminds me to work out, skip some desserts, pray for my family, save money, invest in my marriage, and spend time with my kids.

So let me ask you a question. What is your vision for your family? What do you want your family to look like in a few years? How will all of you interact? What importance will your children place on their relationship with their dad? What will your marriage look like?

If you are going to complete your race—if you are going to persist in times of trouble and hardship—you'll need to know where your finish line is and have the inspiration to keep running. You'll need more than a general idea. You'll need a concrete, specific image of what you want and where you want to wind up.

Dad, your family is counting on you, not only today, but in the future as well. They are counting on you to envision a future for your family, to run your race, and to cross the finish line.

The Takeaway

The key to unlocking the unlimited possibility of your family's potential begins with envisioning the future you desire.

Also by Charles Marshall...

Question: What's better than a magic wand, fairy dust, or good luck?

Answer: The power to take control of your life and improve your situation.

You hold the keys to your success. Use your amazing powers to choose what you want in life, see where your current choices are leading you, and take action to keep your life on course. Charles Marshall shows how to learn from failure, lead with character, and believe when others don't. He provides the inspiration and guidance you need to flourish in every area of your life, including...

- deep and meaningful relationships
- financial responsibility and freedom
- emotional balance and vitality

Question: You are designed to succeed, but are you destined to succeed?

Answer: It's up to you.

To learn more about Harvest House books and
to read sample chapters, visit our website:

www.harvesthousepublishers.com